THE BOOK OF

GRILLING &
BARBECUING

THE BOOK OF

GRILLING & BARBECUING

CECILIA NORMAN

Photography by
Paul Grater

HPBooks
a division of
PRICE STERN SLOAN

ANOTHER BEST SELLING VOLUME FROM HPBOOKS

HPBooks
A division of Price Stern Sloan, Inc.
360 North La Cienega Boulevard
Los Angeles, California 90048
9 8 7 6 5 4 3 2 1

By arrangement with Salamander Books Ltd., and Merehurst Press, London.

This book was created by Merehurst Limited.
5, Great James Street, London WC1N 3DA
Designer: Roger Daniels
Home Economist: Anne Hildyard
Photographer: Paul Grater
Color separation by Kentscan Limited
Printed in Belgium by Proost International Book Production

Library of Congress Cataloging-in-Publication Date

Norman, Cecilia.
    The book of grilling & barbecuing.

    Includes index.
    1. Barbecue cookery. I. Title. II. Title: Book of
grilling and barbecuing.
TX840.B3N665   1988   641.7′6   88-21326
ISBN 0-89586-790-7 (pbk.)

CONTENTS

INTRODUCTION

What can be more relaxing than eating *al fresco* on the patio or in the garden on a balmy night in late spring or early summer? As darkness falls, the grey ashen coals of the barbecue turn to glowing red. The aroma of barbecued food and the smoke wafting upwards stimulates the taste buds and creates a huge appetite. With a glass of wine or a long cool drink, the sumptuous finger-licking steaks, shiny brown sausages or hotly sauced chicken legs taste so much better when eaten outside.

But barbecuing and grilling can be lifted from the mundane choices, and with little additional effort, many imaginative and unusual dishes can be created. Whole Laurier Flounder, page 14, stuffed and cooked in a blanket of bay and vine leaves, Hickory Smoked Chicken, page 62, smoked in a covered barbecue over hickory chips and traditional Greek Souvlakia, page 39, all are wonderful when cooked on the barbecue.

Imaginative vegetables include Hot Hot Aloo, page 78, which is potatoes doused in lime pickle and Sweet & Sour Eggplant, page 79. For dessert choose from Rum & Raisin Persimmons, page 102, filled with a fat-free filling, Hot Tropicanas, page 103, or many others. All are cooked on the grill or barbecue and there are plenty of suggestions for salads, sauces and dips to go with them.

Barbecuing can be a year-round activity. There is even an indoor electric barbecue that is mess-free, which is ideal for winter grilling and barbecuing.

Barbecuing can be a pastime for everyone and is a most informal way of entertaining. Barbecuing does not have to be time consuming and it doesn't have to be greasy. There is nothing to compare with its flavor and whether you want to have a lunch-time cookout or a romantic evening for two, the barbecue's the thing.

EQUIPMENT

There are several different types of barbecues. The choice is yours. Before purchasing, it is a good idea to look at the selection available and decide what type meets your requirements best.

Kettle Barbecues: This barbecue uses charcoal brickettes as fuel. It has its own hood, often with adjustable ducts. It is suitable for all types of barbecuing and can instantly be turned into an oven for cooking of roasts. The advantage of the hood is that if weather is bad, there is some protection while cooking and it prevents spattering and billows of smoke.

Gas Barbecues: These contain lava bricks which heat in the gas flame and absorb juices dripping from the food as it cooks, thus creating flavor. These barbecues ignite almost instantaneously, and require no starter fuel. They retain an even heat and it is possible to have hot coals on one side and moderate on the other when the barbecue has two operational switches. Some are very sophisticated wagon models and all have a gas bottle. The advantage is that you can barbecue at any time of the year. In artic conditions only propane gas is suitable, but normally butane gas is used. The type of barbecue governs the type of gas to be used.

Electric Barbecues: As with the gas grill, these depend on lava bricks to produce an even heat and are usually uncovered. They take about ten minutes to light and must not be used in the rain. The more sophisticated models can be used indoors with suitable ducting. The griddle attachment enables one to fry eggs, burgers, bacon and griddle cakes at the same time.

Smokers: These are specially designed for smoking and most can be used for both dry and wet smoking. You can smoke foods in a regular barbecue by placing a water pan between the food and the coals. The smoke and steam cloud will impregnate the food with flavor. It must be done slowly over several hours and in a covered barbecue.

Accessories: Accessories help for easy barbecuing. Nice to have are a wooden block or table for implements and food, long tools such as tongs and forks as ordinary kitchen tools are not long enough to keep the hands away from the heat source. Various baskets to support the food include rectangular hinged grills and fish-shaped holders. Also needed are brushes for basting, a spit (not necessarily mechanically turned, but it should have a groove on each side of the barbecue), square skewers (round ones cause the food to roll), lots of foil and oven gloves, but not the double-handed kind. Safety requires a fire extinguisher. It is better than a fire blanket in the event of a fire.

Fish-shaped baskets enable whole fish to be turned half way through cooking without damaging them.

Rectangular or square hinged wire baskets are perfect for barbecuing cuts of meats or sliced vegetables.

For barbecuing chunks of meat, fish, vegetable or fruit, use long skewers with either square edges or ridges.

BASIC TECHNIQUES

Charcoal burning barbecues can be ignited in several different ways. Firelighters, liquid starters and gels can be obtained from barbecue centers and hardware stores. Never use paraffin or gas which are highly dangerous and would in any case affect the taste. To achieve flavor, soaked or unsoaked hickory chips can be added to the coals. If soaked, more smoke comes through but the coals tend to sizzle. You can also create additional flavor by sprinkling herbs onto the coals. Seasonings which are herbs impregnated in oil are available and a few drops is all that is necessary.

Before lighting the coals, make certain that your barbecue is in the right position. A heated barbecue is very difficult to move. To start a charcoal fire, spread a single layer of coals over the barbecue base. Pile up the coals and push in a starter. Light and as soon as the fire has caught, spread out the coals. The coals will probably take thirty to forty minutes to get hot enough to begin cooking. When the flames have died down and the charcoal is covered with a white ash, it is time to commence cooking. Lava bricks on the other hand only take a few minutes to heat up sufficiently. Charcoal will burn for about an hour and a half and occasionally brickettes can be added around the edges.

Grilling can be over high, medium or low heat, depending on the type of food. It is easy to adjust gas and electric barbecues, but it is more difficult with the open grill unless you have a kettle with adjustable vents. To test the temperature of the barbecue, carefully place your open hand two to three inches above the coals. If you can keep your hand for five seconds over the coals, the temperature is low. If you can hold it there for about three to four seconds, it is medium. If you can only hold it for two seconds, it is hot. On a covered barbecue, the heat will be greater when the lid is closed. If you want to cook over medium heat and the coals have become too hot, either place the food away from the center of the barbecue and when cooking is completed, push it to the edge to keep warm, or push the coals aside to distribute their heat. To make the fire hotter, push away the ash, push the coals together and gently blow. You can use an inexpensive battery operated fan

There are various methods of cooking on the barbecue and most are interchangeable between the types of barbecue.

Cooking in foil: Food is wrapped in heavy duty or double thicknesses of foil. This prevents the outside of the food from burning before the inside is cooked and keeps all juices trapped inside. For foods that require some browning, make certain there is some space between the covering and the food, otherwise wrap into tight parcels.

Cooking in coals: Food can either be wrapped in foil and dropped into the coals or in some cases even put in without any wrapping.

Rotisserie or Spit Cooking: This method is usually reserved for large pieces of meat which need turning constantly. A basket or roasting rack can be used. Make sure that the meat, and particularly poultry, is securely fixed to the spit. Balance food on the spit for smooth rotation.

Skewers: Most skewered food is marinated first. During cooking the food should be brushed either with an oil, marinade or baste and the skewers must be turned frequently during cooking. Skewers with wooden handles do not get as hot as metal ones. The best ones are very long and can go from one side of the grill, holding two or three servings. Alternatively you can use bamboo skewers for smaller portions, but these need soaking in water for an hour to prevent them from bursting into flames. Oil skewers before use. Serve the food either on the skewers or remove food from the skewers with a fork. Place the skewer on the plate and lower the skewer as the food is removed.

Smoke Cooking: No water bath is needed to dry smoke, generally the method used for fish. Smoked poultry is more often cooked over a water bath above the coals but underneath the food. This may require two racks. A covered barbecue is essential for smoke cooking.

Grilling: All barbecues can be used for grilling. Most recipes can also be cooked under an ordinary grill, although the flavor is lacking.

Roasting: Roasting is done in a covered barbecue or by tenting the food with foil. When roasting the food is much thicker then when grilling. The heat is lost on the top surface and food needs to be turned much more frequently.

Cooking times: Although times are given in the book, they are a guide only. There are so many variables due to the thickness of the food, the type and heat of the coals, etc., that accuracy cannot be guaranteed. One of the great pleasures of barbecuing is that it is not a precise science and it gives the chef room to let his individuality roam free.

GRILLING GUIDE TO MEAT & POULTRY

	Total Time	Grill Heat
CHOPS		
Lamb Chops	15 mins.	Medium
Pork Chops	30-40 mins.	Medium
Rib Chops	1 hour	Low
STEAKS		
Rare	10 mins.	Hot
Medium	15 mins.	Hot
Well Done	20 mins.	Hot
ROASTS		
Beef	2-3 hours	Low
Lamb	2-1/2 to 3-1/2 hours	Low
Pork	20 mins. per lb.	Low
BURGERS		
Thin	8-10 mins.	Hot
Thick	12-15 mins.	Medium
SAUSAGES		
Beef	10-15 mins.	Medium
Pork	15-20 mins.	Medium
Frankfurters	5-10 mins.	Medium
Cocktail	4-6 mins.	Medium
POULTRY		
Whole chicken	20-30 mins. per lb.	Medium
Chicken quarters	20-30 mins.	Medium
Drumsticks	20-25 mins.	Medium

MARINADES & BASTES

RICH TOMATO BASTE

1 large red bell pepper, seeded, finely chopped
1 lb. firm tomatoes, peeled, finely chopped
1 small onion, finely chopped
1 garlic clove, finely chopped
2/3 cup dry white wine
1 teaspoon fresh rosemary leaves
Pinch sugar
Salt and freshly ground black pepper to taste
2 tablespoons sunflower oil

Combine all ingredients except oil, salt and pepper in a large saucepan. Bring to a boil. Simmer, uncovered, until sauce thickens. Purée in a blender. Season with salt and pepper and mix in oil. Makes 1-1/4 cups.

COGNAC MARINADE

1/4 cup brandy
2/3 cup dry white wine
2 tablespoons olive oil
2 ozs. button mushrooms, finely sliced
2 shallots, peeled, finely chopped
1 teaspoon fresh thyme leaves
4 bay leaves
1 small garlic clove, crushed
10 black peppercorns, crushed
1 teaspoon salt

Combine all ingredients in a small bowl. Cover and refrigerate 24 hours. Strain before serving. Makes 1-1/4 cups.

SWEET & SOUR MARINADE

Grated peel and juice 1 medium-size orange
2/3 cup honey
2/3 cup red wine vinegar
3 tablespoons soy sauce
3 tablespoons Worcestershire sauce
1 tablespoon sesame oil

Combine all ingredients in a small saucepan. Bring to a boil, then simmer, uncovered, 5 minutes or until sauce is reduced by about one-third. Makes 1-1/4 cups.

—— MARINADES & BASTES ——

WARMLY SPICED MARINADE

1/4 cup plus 1 tablespoon dark-brown sugar
2 tablespoons red wine vinegar
1 cup water
1/4 teaspoon ground cloves
1/4 teaspoon dry mustard
1-1/2 teaspoons ground allspice
1 tablespoon cornstarch
1 small Delicious apple, peeled, cored, finely chopped

Combine all ingredients in a small saucepan. Bring to a boil, stirring continuously. Simmer 5 minutes or until sauce has thickened. Makes 1-1/4 cups.

FIERY CHILI BASTE

2/3 cup water
2 tablespoons dark-brown sugar
2/3 cup ketchup
3/4 cup cider vinegar
2 tablespoons Worcestershire sauce
2 teaspoons chili powder
1/4 onion, finely chopped

Combine water and brown sugar in small heavy saucepan. Stir until dissolved. Add remaining ingredients. Bring to a boil. Simmer over low heat until sauce is reduced by about one-third. Makes 1-1/4 cups.

CITRUS MARINADE

Juice and grated peel 4 limes
Juice and grated peel 1 lemon
2 teaspoons salt
1/4 cup plus 2 tablespoons sunflower oil
12 white peppercorns, crushed

Mix all ingredients in a small bowl. Cover and refrigerate 8 hours or overnight. Strain before using. Makes 1-1/4 cups.

Whole Laurier Flounder

1 lb. flounder, cleaned
20 bay leaves
Olive oil
10 grape leaves, soaked, drained
2 lemons, cut in half, and fresh flat-leaf parsley
    sprigs to garnish

Stuffing:
2 cups soft bread crumbs
1/4 cup butter, melted
2 teaspoons fresh lemon juice
1 teaspoon grated lemon peel
2 teaspoons chopped fresh parsley
Salt and freshly ground black pepper to taste
1/4 cup finely chopped peeled cooked shrimp
1 egg, beaten

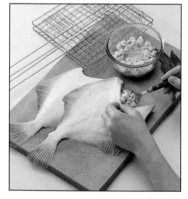

Remove and discard fish heads. Cut a slit along stomachs of fish to form pockets. Lift flesh away from bone. To prepare stuffing, combine all stuffing ingredients in a large bowl.

Spoon stuffing into pockets. Insert 3 or 4 bay leaves over stuffing in each fish to hold in place. Brush fish with olive oil.

Oil grape leaves. Line a hinged meat grill with oiled grape leaves. Arrange remaining bay leaves on grape leaves. Place fish on bay leaves. Cook fish in grill on a rack over medium coals 10 to 15 minutes per side or until fish is done, basting occasionally with olive oil. Garnish with lemon and parsley sprigs. Makes 4 servings.

Red Mullet with Fennel Seeds

1/4 cup vegetable oil
1 teaspoon fresh lemon juice
1 teaspoon fennel seeds, crushed
1/4 teaspoon sea salt
1/4 teaspoon freshly ground black pepper
1/2 lb. red mullet
Fresh fennel leaves to garnish

To prepare marinade, combine oil, lemon juice, fennel seeds, sea salt and pepper in a large shallow dish.

Rinse fish, drain and wipe dry with paper towels. Cut slits through fish skin twice on each side. Place fish in marinade. Refrigerate 1 hour, basting occasionally.

Drain fish. Cook on an oiled rack over hot coals 6 to 8 minutes on each side, basting occasionally with marinade to prevent sticking and encourage browning. Garnish with fennel leaves. Makes 4 servings.

Louisiana Angels

9 slices bacon
18 small mushrooms
1/2 cup butter
2 tablespoons fresh lemon juice
3 tablespoons chopped fresh parsley
Pinch cayenne pepper
18 medium-size oysters, shucked, 6 shells
　　reserved
Cornstarch
Fresh flat-leaf parsley sprigs to garnish

On a cutting board, stretch bacon slightly with back of a knife. Cut in half crosswise. In a large skillet, lightly fry bacon until opaque and still limp. Drain on paper towels.

Bring a medium-size saucepan of water to a boil. Blanch mushrooms 1 minute. Drain on paper towels. Melt butter in a small saucepan, but do not clarify. Remove from heat. Stir in lemon juice, chopped parsley and cayenne pepper. Keep warm. Dust oysters with cornstarch. Wrap bacon around oysters. Thread wrapped oysters alternately with mushrooms onto 4 to 6 skewers, spearing wrapped oysters through "eye" of oysters to keep in position on skewer.

Brush oysters and mushrooms generously with seasoned butter. Cook on a rack over medium coals 3 to 5 minutes or until oysters are just brown. Do not overcook or oysters will toughen. Remove oysters and mushrooms from skewers and serve in reserved shells. Spoon remaining seasoned butter on top. Garnish with parsley sprigs. Makes 6 servings.

Luxury Ginger Scampi

2/3 cup vegetable oil
Grated peel and juice 1 small lemon
1/4 cup plus 2 tablespoons soy sauce
1 garlic clove, crushed
1 teaspoon finely grated gingerroot
1/2 teaspoon ground marjoram
1-1/2 lbs. fresh or frozen peeled jumbo shrimp,
    thawed if frozen, deveined
Fresh marjoram sprigs and lemon twists to
    garnish

To prepare marinade, combine oil, lemon
peel and juice, soy sauce, garlic, gingerroot
and marjoram in a large bowl.

Stir shrimp into marinade. Refrigerate 2
hours, basting occasionally,

Thread shrimp crosswise onto 6 skewers.
Cook on a rack over hot coals 7 to 10 minutes
or until shrimp are opaque, turning frequently. Garnish with marjoram sprigs and lemon
twists and serve at once. Makes 6 servings.

Simply Grilled Lobster

2 (2-lb.) freshly cooked lobsters
1/2 cup butter, softened
2 teaspoons fresh lemon juice
Salt and black pepper to taste
Lemon wedges and fresh flat-leaf parsley
   sprigs to garnish

Split lobsters in half by cutting lengthwise along line down back and through tail. Crack claws. Remove gills, greyish sack near head and black vein which runs lengthwise along tail.

Remove coral. Beat with 1/2 of butter. Sprinkle lobster flesh with lemon juice and season lightly with salt and pepper. Melt remaining butter in a small saucepan. Brush lobster flesh generously with melted butter.

Cook lobster flesh side up on an oiled rack over medium coals 5 to 10 minutes. Turn over and cook 3 to 4 minutes more or until lobster flesh is hot and browning slightly. Top with coral butter and garnish with lemon wedges and parsley sprigs. Makes 4 servings.

Aromatic Grilled Salmon

6 (6-oz.) salmon steaks
Salt and freshly ground black pepper to taste
All-purpose flour
1/2 cup butter
Handful winter savory or 1 to 2 tablespoons
 dried winter savory, moistened
2 tablespoons lump fish caviar
Fresh winter savory sprigs to garnish

Rinse steaks and pat dry on paper towels. Season with salt and pepper. Dip into flour and shake off surplus.

Melt butter in a small saucepan and brush over steaks. Place steaks in a hinged grill. Sprinkle winter savory over coals when hot.

Cook steaks in grill on a rack over hot coals 45 minutes or until center bone removes easily, turning once during cooking. Baste occasionally with melted butter. Should steaks brown too quickly, reduce heat or move grill to side of rack. Top with caviar and garnish with savory sprigs. Makes 6 servings.

Scallops with Tindooris

2 lbs. fresh or frozen scallops, thawed if frozen
12 tindooris
2/3 cup olive oil
1 tablespoon fresh lemon juice
1 tablespoon fresh lime juice
1/2 teaspoon lemon pepper
1/4 teaspoon onion salt
Lemon and lime slices to garnish

Remove any dark veins from scallops. Rinse and pat dry with paper towels. Rinse tindooris and cut in half lengthwise. Bring a saucepan of water to fast boil. Add tindooris and cook 1 minute. Drain and cool.

To prepare marinade, combine olive oil, lemon and lime juices, lemon pepper and onion salt in a large bowl. Stir scallops into marinade. Refrigerate 45 to 60 minutes, gently stirring occasionally. Add tindooris during last 15 minutes.

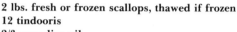

Oil 6 to 8 skewers. Thread scallops and tindooris onto oiled skewers. Cook on a rack over medium coals 5 to 10 minutes or until scallops are opaque, basting frequently with marinade. Garnish with lemon and lime slices. Makes 6 to 8 servings.

Note: Tindooris are a vegetable about the size of a gherkin pickle. They have smooth dark-green skin and a texture similar to zucchini. They can be obtained from Asian stores and supermarkets stocking exotic vegetables. If unavailable, substitute zucchini.

Swordfish Kebabs

2 lbs. swordfish, skinned, boned
Juice 2 lemons
2 medium-size onions
18 cherry tomatoes
2/3 cup olive oil
1/2 teaspoon garlic salt
1/2 teaspoon freshly ground black pepper
1/2 cup finely chopped fresh chives
1/2 cup finely chopped fresh parsley
Lemon wedges and fresh flat-leaf parsley
    sprigs to garnish

Cut fish in 1-1/2-inch cubes. In a small bowl, combine fish and juice of 1 lemon. Refrigerate 1 hour, turning once.

Cut onions in half. Remove centers, leaving a 3 layer wall. Separate layers, cutting each in half. Curve to form a cone. Alternately thread fish cubes, onion cones and cherry tomatoes onto 6 skewers. To prepare oil baste, combine remaining lemon juice, olive oil, garlic salt and pepper in a small bowl. Brush over kebabs.

Cook on a rack over medium coals 10 to 15 minutes, turning frequently and brushing with oil baste. Combine chives and chopped parsley on a flat surface. Roll hot kebabs in herb mixture. Garnish with lemon wedges and parsley sprigs. Makes 6 servings.

Mackerel with Rhubarb Sauce

6 medium-size fresh mackerel, cleaned
Salt and freshly ground black pepper to taste
Vegetable oil
Lemon twists to garnish

Rhubarb Sauce:
1/2 lb. trimmed rhubarb
1 teaspoon fresh lemon juice
1/4 cup sweet apple cider
3 tablespoons light-brown sugar
1/8 teaspoon ground nutmeg

Season inside of fish with salt and pepper. Brush all over with oil.

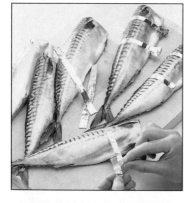

Fold 2 double thicknesses of foil in 2 (4" x 1/2") strips. Wrap around fish, placing 1 strip near top of fish and other in center. Fold open ends twice to achieve a snug fit. This will form a flat loop to enable fish to be handled easily.

To prepare Rhubarb Sauce, combine rhubarb, lemon juice, apple cider, brown sugar and nutmeg in a small saucepan. Simmer until rhubarb is very soft, shaking pan occasionally. Purée in a blender and return to pan. Cover and keep sauce hot. Cook fish on a rack over medium coals 7 to 10 minutes on each side or until juices run clear when deeply pricked. Brush frequently with oil. Use foil loops to help turn fish carefully. Garnish with lemon twists. Serve with Rhubarb Sauce. Makes 6 servings.

Pink Grapefruit Trout

6 small trout, cleaned
4 small pink grapefruit
1-1/4 cups dry white wine
4 green onions, finely sliced
16 black peppercorns, lightly crushed
2 tablespoons whipping cream
1/3 cup butter
Salt to taste
Fresh flat-leaf parsley sprigs to garnish

Place each trout on an oiled double thickness of foil large enough to loosely wrap trout.

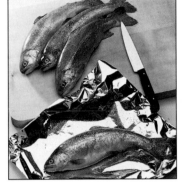

To prepare sauce, thinly peel 1 grapefruit and finely shred peel. Place shredded peel in a small saucepan. Cover with cold water. Bring to a boil and cook 3 to 4 minutes or until soft. Drain well. Remove pith, membranes, seeds and segments from peeled grapefruit. Reserve segments for garnish. Finely grate peel and squeeze juice from remaining 3 grapefruit. In a medium-size saucepan, combine grapefruit peel and juice, wine, green onions and peppercorns. Simmer 10 to 15 minutes or until 2/3 cup of liquid remains.

Remove from heat. Add whipping cream and butter. Stir until butter is melted. Strain into a medium-size bowl. Season with salt and mix in softened peel. Pour a small amount of sauce over each trout. Fold up foil, leaving a 1-inch space over trout for steam to circulate. Cook on a rack over hot coals 20 minutes; do not turn foil packets over. Garnish with reserved grapefruit segments and parsley sprigs. Serve with remaining sauce. Makes 6 servings.

Mediterranean Shrimp

2 lemons and 1/2 cucumber to garnish
Juice 1 large lemon
2/3 cup vegetable oil
18 fresh or frozen unpeeled jumbo shrimp,
**   thawed if frozen**

Cut top and bottom from lemons. Slice middle sections thinly. Using a zester, remove strips of cucumber skin lengthwise. Thinly slice cucumber. Curve cucumber slices around lemon slices and thread onto wooden picks.

Pour lemon juice into a shallow dish and oil into another. Dip 2 or 3 shrimp into lemon juice. Shake off excess, then dip into oil. Repeat with remaining shrimp.

Cook shrimp on a rack over hot coals 10 to 12 minutes, brushing frequently with remaining oil. Garnish with lemon and cucumber slices and serve hot. Makes 6 servings.

Tarama Trout

6 small trout
2 tablespoons lemon juice
Black pepper to taste
1/2 cup taramasalata
Fresh flat-leaf parsley sprigs to garnish

Clean trout, rinse and blot on paper towels until dry.

Brush inside of trout with lemon juice. Season with pepper. Carefully fill cavities with taramasalata.

Place trout in a hinged grill. Cook over hot coals 3 to 4 minutes on each side. Garnish with parsley sprigs. Makes 6 servings.

Trout in Saffron Fumet

6 small rainbow trout, cleaned
1-3/4 cups cold water
6 black peppercorns
1/2 celery stalk, coarsely chopped
1 fresh parsley sprig
1 bay leaf
1 fresh thyme sprig
3 thick slices carrot
1 shallot, peeled, coarsely chopped
1/4 teaspoon salt
2 teaspoons white wine vinegar
1/2 cup dry white wine
1/2 teaspoon powdered saffron
1/3 cup butter
Fresh celery leaves to garnish

Remove heads and tails from trout and reserve for fumet.

Slit each trout along belly. Open trout and place open edges down on a flat surface. Press with thumbs along backbone to flatten. Open trout and lift out backbone. In a large saucepan, combine reserved heads and tails, cold water, peppercorns, chopped celery, parsley, bay leaf, thyme, carrot, shallot, salt, wine vinegar and wine. Bring to a boil, then remove scum. Reduce heat, cover tightly and simmer 30 minutes. Strain liquor through a fine nylon sieve into a large bowl. Return to saucepan, add saffron and boil vigorously uncovered until reduced to 3/4 cup. Cool.

Place trout flesh-side down in a large shallow dish. Pour saffron fumet over trout and refrigerate 30 minutes. Melt butter in a small saucepan and brush over trout. Cook in hinged grills over hot coals 2 to 3 minutes on each side. Garnish with celery leaves. Makes 6 servings.

Smoked Red Snapper

1-1/2 lbs. red snapper, bream or carp, cleaned
1/2 cup sea salt
4 cups water
2 handfuls hickory chips
Olive oil
Fresh fennel leaves and radish flowers to
garnish

Place fish in a large shallow dish. Dissolve sea salt in water. Pour over fish and refrigerate 30 minutes.

Drain fish thoroughly. Place on a wire rack and let stand about 2-1/2 hours or until dry to touch. Meanwhile, soak hickory chips in water 30 minutes. Using a covered barbecue, push coals to one side and ignite. When coals have burned down to a white ash stage, drain hickory chips and add to white ashes.

Thoroughly brush fish with olive oil and place on a rack away from coals. Close lid and cook 30 to 45 minutes or until fish flakes when tested with a fork, turning over once during cooking. Serve hot or cold. Garnish with fennel leaves and radish flowers. Makes 4 to 6 servings.

Note: This tastes particularly good served with Fennel Salad, page 114.

Halibut Steaks with Dill

4 to 6 sprigs fresh dill
1/2 cup mayonnaise
Salt and freshly ground black pepper to taste
3 or 4 (1-inch-thick) halibut steaks
About 1/3 cup yellow cornmeal
Fresh dill sprigs to garnish

Strip feathery leaves of dill from stalk. In a small bowl, combine dill leaves and mayonnaise. Season to taste with salt and pepper. Mix well.

Spread both sides of each steak with seasoned mayonnaise, then dip into cornmeal to lightly coat.

Cook steaks on a rack over hot coals 10 to 15 minutes or until steaks are opaque and flake when tested with a fork, turning once during cooking. Surface of cooked steaks should be golden-brown. If browning occurs before fish is cooked through, reduce heat or move to edge of rack to finish cooking. Garnish with dill. Makes 4 to 6 servings.

Crab Stuffed Fish Cakes

1-1/2 lbs. minced white fish
1 small onion, very finely chopped
About 1/4 cup matzo meal
1 tablespoon ground almonds
Salt and freshly ground black pepper to taste
1 egg, beaten
1/4 cup crabmeat
Fresh flat-leaf parsley sprigs to garnish

To coat:
2 eggs, beaten
1/4 cup matzo meal
Sunflower oil

In a large bowl, combine fish, onion, 1/4 cup of matzo meal and ground almonds. Season with salt and pepper. Mix well.

Mix in egg, adding more matzo meal if necessary to form a mixture which holds together. Shape in 16 balls. Sprinkle a flat surface with matzo meal. Flatten balls with palm of hand on flat surface. Place 1 teaspoon of crabmeat in center of each flattened ball. Wrap flattened balls around crabmeat to reform balls. Press down lightly to fishcake shapes. To coat, dip fishcakes into beaten eggs, then in matzo meal. Brush both sides of fishcakes with sunflower oil.

Cook on a rack over hot coals 6 to 8 minutes on each side. Garnish with parsley sprigs. Makes 6 to 8 servings.

Note: Serve with Cucumber Raita, page 105.

Ploughman's Burgers

3 eggs
1/2 teaspoon freshly ground black pepper
3 lbs. lean ground beef
4 to 6 tablespoon chutney
8 ozs. Emmenthal cheese, thinly sliced
Shredded lettuce

Beat eggs in a large bowl. Mix in pepper and ground meat.

Shape in 24 thin patties. Spread 1/2 of patties with chutney, leaving a border so that chutney does not quite reach edges.

Cut out 12 circles of cheese smaller than patties. Lay slices of cheese over sauce, topping with cheese trimmings. Cover with remaining patties and press edges together to seal. Cook on a rack over hot coals 8 to 10 minute on each side or to desired doneness. Garnish with lettuce. Makes 12 servings.

Note: This is good served with Potters Red Relish, page 106.

Fillet Steak Envelopes

4 (6-oz.) beef fillet steaks
1 (6-oz.) veal cutlet
1/2 cup butter, softened
4 garlic cloves, crushed
1 teaspoon dried leaf basil
Salt and freshly ground black pepper to taste

Using a rolling pin, flatten steaks to 1/2 inch thick between sheets of waxed paper. Pound veal to 1/4-inch thick and cut in 4 pieces.

Using a sharp knife, cut a deep horizontal slit through each steak to form a pocket. In a small bowl, mix butter, garlic and basil. Season with salt and pepper. Mix well. Spread 1/2 of seasoned butter inside pockets, then insert a veal piece into each pocket.

Spread outside of steaks with remaining seasoned butter. Cook on a rack over hot coals 2 minutes on each side to seal. Position steaks away from heat. Cook over medium coals to desired doneness, see page 11, turning steaks over occasionally. Makes 4 servings.

Note: Serve with Crispy Potato Skins, page 112 and Watercress Salad, page 113.

Danish Patties

6 ozs. pork tenderloin
6 ozs. cooked ham
6 ozs. Danish salami, rind removed
Fresh flat-leaf parsley sprigs to garnish

Dough:
3 cups all-purpose flour
Pinch salt
1 teaspoon baking powder
1/4 cup vegetable shortening
2/3 cup milk

Generously grease 12 pieces of double thicknesses of foil. Using a food processor fitted with a metal blade, process pork, ham and salami until finely chopped.

To prepare dough, sift flour, salt and baking powder into a large bowl. Using a pastry blender or 2 knives, cut in shortening until pieces are size of peas. Add milk and mix to a soft dough. Divide dough in 12 balls. On a lightly floured surface, flatten each ball in a 5-inch circle. Spoon an equal quantity of meat filling onto center of each circle. Dampen edges of dough and pull edges to top. Press well to seal. Flatten slightly with palm of hand.

Place 1 patty seam-side down on each piece of greased foil, flattening slightly with palm of hand. Wrap and seal securely. Cook over medium coals about 10 minutes or until filling is completely cooked, turning foil packets over once during cooking. To test filling for doneness, insert a sharp tipped knife into center of patties. No juices should escape. Garnish with sprigs. Makes 12 servings.

Pita Burgers

2 eggs, beaten
1 teaspoon turmeric
1 teaspoon ground cumin
1/4 teaspoon cayenne pepper
2 garlic cloves, very finely chopped
2 lbs. lean ground beef
2 cups fresh bread crumbs
8 pitted green olives, chopped
6 pita breads, cut in half
Red leaf lettuce leaves and sliced stuffed green
    olives to garnish

In a large bowl, beat eggs, turmeric, cumin,
cayenne pepper and garlic.

Mix ground meat, bread crumbs and
chopped olives into egg mixture. Shape in 12
patties. Cook on a rack over hot coals 8 to 10
minutes on each side or to desired doneness.

When patties are almost done, warm pita
breads on side of rack. Open each pita bread
and insert a pattie. Garnish with lettuce leaves
and sliced olives. Makes 12 servings.

Beef & Bacon Satay

3/4 lb. beef sirloin tip
3/4 lb. lean bacon
1 medium-size onion, finely chopped
Grated peel and juice 2 lemons
1/4 cup ground coriander
2 tablespoons ground cumin
1-1/2 cups crunchy peanut butter
1/2 cup walnut oil
2 tablespoons honey
18 wooden skewers
4 medium-size zucchini

Cut beef in 1-inch cubes. Place in a large shallow dish. Cut bacon in half lengthwise.

Stretch bacon slices on a flat surface with a round-bladed knife drawn flat along slices. Roll each slice up tightly along its length. Place in dish with cubed beef. In a small bowl, combine onion, lemon peel and juice, coriander, cumin, peanut butter, walnut oil and honey. Pour over beef and bacon. Refrigerate at least 1 hour, basting meat occasionally.

Meanwhile, soak skewers in water 1 hour. Peel zucchini. Cut in half lengthwise, then cut in 1/2-inch chunks. Alternately thread beef cubes, bacon rolls and zucchini chunks onto soaked skewers. Cook on a rack over hot coals about 20 minutes or to desired doneness, turning frequently. Makes 6 servings.

Note: Serve with cooked white rice and garnish with green onion flowers and fresh flat-leaf parsley sprigs.

Lamb Kumquat Kebabs

2 large oranges
1-1/4 lbs. lean boneless lamb
1 cup cooked short-grain rice
8 to 10 fresh mint leaves
Salt and freshly ground black pepper to taste
15 kumquats, rinsed, stems removed
Olive oil
Fresh mint sprigs to garnish

Sauce:
1 cup fresh orange juice
1 teaspoon cornstarch
1/2 teaspoon paprika
2 teaspoons Cointreau or other orange-flavored
    liqueur
1 teaspoon maple syrup

Squeeze juice from oranges. If necessary, add enough water to make 1 cup liquid.

Remove orange peel and snip with scissors. Cut lamb in 1-inch cubes. Using a food processor fitted with a metal blade, process orange peel, lamb cubes, rice and mint leaves to a smooth paste. Season with salt and pepper. Mix well. If necessary, process in 2 batches. Divide meat paste in 20 balls. Shape 4 balls of meat paste around skewers, alternating with 3 kumquats.

To prepare sauce, blend 1 cup orange juice and cornstarch in a small saucepan. Bring to a boil and cook until sauce thickens, stirring constantly. Stir in paprika, Cointreau and maple syrup. Keep warm. Cook kebabs on a rack over hot coals 10 to 12 minutes or to desired doneness, turning skewers frequently and basting with olive oil. Coat kebabs with sauce. Remove skewers from lamb balls and kumquats. Garnish with mint sprigs. Makes 5 servings.

Ham Steaks with Plum Sauce

1 lb. purple plums
1/4 cup honey
1/4 cup port wine
1 tablespoon plus 1 teaspoon sunflower oil
4 (5-oz.) ham steaks
Red leaf lettuce leaves, fresh flat-leaf parsley
    sprigs and curly endive to garnish

To prepare sauce, cook plums gently in a covered medium-size saucepan until plums are very soft. Strain plums and juice through a nylon sieve set over a large bowl. Press with back of a wooden spoon until pulp and juice are extracted. Discard skin and pits.

Warm honey in a bowl set over a pan of hot water. Stir in plum plup with juice, port wine and sunflower oil. Set bowl over hot water to keep sauce liquified while cooking steaks.

Cut edges of steaks to prevent curling during cooking. Coat steaks thickly with sauce. Cook on a rack over hot coals about 5 minutes on each side or until heated through, basting frequently with sauce. Garnish with lettuce leaves, parsley sprigs, and endive. Makes 4 servings.

Jewelled Pork Chops

3 shallots
1/2 small red bell pepper
1/2 small green bell pepper
1-1/2 ozs. pistachio nuts
4 to 6 (1-inch-thick) pork chops
2 tablespoons walnut oil
2 teaspoons fresh lemon juice
Salt and freshly ground black pepper to taste
6 tiny pearl onions
3 gherkin pickles, cut in half
6 pitted fresh black cherries

Peel and coarsely chop shallots. Seed and finely dice bell peppers. Cut nuts in half.

In a medium-size bowl, cover shallots, bell peppers and nuts with boiling water. Let stand 10 minutes, then drain.

Using tip of a sharp knife, make several small slits into both sides of chops. Insert pieces of shallots, bell peppers and nuts into slits. In a 1-cup measure, combine walnut oil and lemon juice. Brush both sides of chops. Season with salt and pepper. Cook on a rack over medium coals 10 to 12 minutes on each side or until no longer pink in center, basting occasionally with oil mixture. Thread pearl onions, pickles and cherries onto wooden picks and serve with pork chops. Makes 4 to 6 servings.

Juniper Crown Roast

1 small onion, finely chopped
3 tablespoons butter
1/2 cup hot well-seasoned beef stock
1 cup soft bread crumbs
2 tablespons finely chopped dried apricots
8 juniper berries, finely ground
1 (2-lb.) crown roast of lamb

To prepare stuffing, in a medium-size saucepan, saute onion in butter until onion is transparent. Remove from heat. Mix in hot beef stock, bread crumbs, apricots and juniper berries. Stir to form a soft but manageable mixture. Letstand 10 minutes.

Generously oil a large circle of a double thickness of foil. Place crown roast bone ends up on oiled foil. Press stuffing into center cavity.

Cook over medium coals in a covered barbecue about 30 minutes or to desired doneness. If using an uncovered barbecue, tent with foil to enclose crown roast and cook about 50 minutes or to desired doneness. If desired, place a cutlet frill over each bone before serving. Makes 4 to 5 servings.

Note: Serve with Capered New Potatoes, page 76, garnished with fresh flat-leaf parsley sprigs.

Souvlakia

1-1/2 lbs. lean boneless lamb
1-1/2 tablespoons sea salt
1/4 cup plus 2 tablespoons chopped fresh
    oregano leaves
1/4 cup olive oil
Fresh bay leaves
1 large onion, finely chopped
6 to 8 cherry tomatoes, cut in half
1 small cucumber, peeled, thinly sliced
2 lemons, cut in wedges
1-1/4 cups plain yogurt
Fresh oregano sprigs to garnish

Cut lamb in 1-inch cubes and toss in sea salt.

In a small bowl, mix 1/4 cup of chopped oregano leaves with olive oil. Thread lamb and bay
leaves onto skewers, leaving generous gaps
between lamb cubes to allow heat to per-
meate. Brush with oil mixture.

Cook on a rack over hot coals 20 minutes or to
desired doneness, turning skewers occasionally. Arrange onion, cherry tomatoes,
cucumber and lemons in sections on individual plates. Spoon yogurt on 1 side.
Sprinkle with remaining oregano leaves.
Using a fork, remove lamb from skewers. Arrange across vegetables. Garnish with oregano sprigs. Makes 4 to 5 servings.

— Claret & Green Peppercorn Steaks —

1-1/4 cups claret wine
1/2 cup olive oil
2 tablespoons green peppercorns, ground
2 tablespoons coriander seeds
6 to 8 (1-inch-thick) beef strip steaks, trimmed
Fresh flat-leaf parsley sprigs and fresh
    marjoram sprigs to garnish
Sour cream

To prepare marinade, combine wine, olive oil, ground peppercorns and coriander seeds in a large bowl.

Pierce steaks deeply, then immerse in marinade. Refrigerate at least 2 hours.

Cook steaks on a rack over hot coals 1 minute on each side to seal. Continue cooking to desired doneness, see page 11, turning steaks over occasionally and basting frequently with marinade. Garnish with parsley and marjoram sprigs. Serve with a dollop of sour cream. Makes 6 to 8 servings.

Note: Resilience and firmness are good indications of doneness—the more done, the firmer the steak will be when pressed with a knife handle.

Mini Roasts

1 (2-1/2-lb.) rolled beef roast
1 medium-size red onion, coarsely chopped
1 small green bell pepper, seeded, chopped
1 Green Delicious apple, peeled, cored
    chopped
1-1/4 cups beef stock
2 tablespoons olive oil
2 tablespoons red currant jelly
1 tablespoon tomato paste
1 tablespoon Worcestershire sauce
1 teaspoon cornstarch
1 tablespoon crushed lemon verbena leaves
Fresh flat-leaf parsley sprigs to garnish

Untie roast and cut through grain in 4 pieces. Remove fat and cut fat in 4 strips. Shape each piece of meat in a roll by rolling with hands on a flat surface. Place 1 strip of fat lengthwise down 1 side of each roll. Tie each roll with string and place in a medium-size dish.

To prepare marinade, combine remaining ingredients in a medium-size saucepan. Bring to a boil, stirring occasionally, then simmer 10 minutes or until reduced by one-fourth. Cool marinade and pour over beef rolls. Refrigerate 12 hours. Cook on an oiled rack over hot coals about 20 minutes or to desired doneness if using a covered barbecue. Or if using an uncovered barbecue, cook 35 to 40 minutes or to desired doneness. Turn beef frequently and baste with remaining marinade. Garnish with parsley sprigs. Makes 4 to 8 servings.

Note: Serve on wooden platters with Skewered Potato Crisps, page 86, and Potters Red Relish, page 106.

Frankfurters with Mustard Dip

3 tablespoons dry mustard
1 cup half and half
12 to 16 frankfurters
Salt and freshly ground black pepper to taste
12 to 16 hot dog rolls, if desired

To prepare dip, blend dry mustard and half and half in a small bowl. Cover and refrigerate 15 minutes.

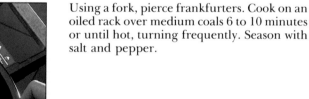

Using a fork, pierce frankfurters. Cook on an oiled rack over medium coals 6 to 10 minutes or until hot, turning frequently. Season with salt and pepper.

Wrap foil around 1 end of each frankfurter. Arrange on a serving platter with a bowl of dip in center. If desired, insert frankfurters into hot dog rolls and spread with dip. Makes 12 to 16 servings.

Caribbean Burgers

2 tablespoons vegetable oil
1 large onion, finely chopped
1 garlic clove, crushed
1 green bell pepper, seeded, finely chopped
2 lbs. lean ground beef
1 teaspoon dried mixed herbs
2 eggs, beaten
2 cups fresh bread crumbs
1 tablespoon tomato paste
Salt and freshly ground black pepper to taste
1 small pineapple, peeled, thinly cut in 12
   slices
Melted butter
Fresh herbs to garnish

Heat oil in a small saucepan. Add onion, garlic and bell pepper and saute 5 minutes or until soft.

In a large bowl, combine sauteed vegetables, ground beef, mixed herbs, eggs, bread crumbs and tomato paste. Season with salt and pepper. Mix well. Shape in 12 patties. Cook on an oiled rack over hot coals 8 to 10 minutes on each side or to desired doneness.

Brush pineapple rings on both sides with melted butter. Cook on rack over hot coals 3 to 6 minutes or until golden brown, turning once. Top each burger with a pineapple ring. Garnish with fresh herbs. Makes 12 servings.

Note: Serve with Singed Spiced Plaintains, page 82.

Calf Liver Kebabs

2 lbs. calf liver
1/4 cup plus 2 tablespoons dry red wine
1/4 cup plus 2 tablespoons sunflower oil
1 tablespoon Dijon-style mustard
1/2 teaspoon onion salt
1/2 teaspoon black pepper
3/4 lb. small fresh mushrooms
Cooked spaghetti, if desired
Fresh herbs to garnish

Cut liver in 1-1/2-inch chunks.

To prepare marinade, combine wine, sunflower oil, mustard, onion salt and pepper in a large bowl. Add liver and mushrooms. Mix throroughly to coat. Refrigerate at least 1 hour, turning occasionally.

Alternately thread liver and mushrooms onto skewers. Cook on a rack over hot coals 10 to 15 minutes, turning skewers frequently and basting with marinade. Do not overcook or liver will become dry and tough. Serve on spaghetti, if desired. Garnish with fresh herbs. Makes 6 to 8 servings.

Oriental Spare Ribs

6 lbs. lean pork spare ribs
1/2 cup hoisin sauce
1/2 miso paste
1-1/4 cups tomato paste
1-1/2 teaspoons ground ginger
1-1/2 teaspoons five-spice powder
1-1/8 cups dark-brown sugar
3 garlic cloves, crushed
1 teaspoon salt
2 tablespoons saki (rice wine) or dry sherry
Green onion stems and curls to garnish

Separate ribs and trim away most of fat.

To prepare sauce, combine remaining ingredients in a large bowl. Place ribs in a large shallow pan or dish. Spread sauce over ribs. Refrigerate remaining sauce. Cover ribs and refrigerate at least 4 hours or overnight.

Place a drip pan in medium coals. Cook ribs on a rack 45 to 60 minutes or until tender, turning occasionally and basting with sauce. Meanwhile, heat remaining sauce gently. Garnish ribs with green onion stems and curls and serve with sauce. Makes 8 servings.

Note: If desired, offer warmed moist finger towels for cleanup.

Sausage with Horseradish Dip

3 tablespoons grated horseradish
1/2 (4-oz.) pkg. cream cheese
2 tablespoons fresh lemon juice
1/2 teaspoon sugar
1/2 teaspoon salt
2/3 cup dairy sour cream
8 to 12 thick low-fat pork or beef sausages
Vegetable oil

To made dip, blend horseradish, cream cheese, lemon juice, sugar and salt in a medium-size bowl. Gradually stir in sour cream. Cover and refrigerate.

Prick sausages with a fork. Thread onto skewers. Brush with oil. Cook on a rack over medium coals 12 to 15 minutes or until cooked through, turning skewers frequently.

Arrange hot sausages in a circle on a wooden platter and place bowl of dip in center. Makes 4 to 6 servings.

Note: If desired, serve with Cos lettuce and radishes.

—————— Brochettes Mexicana ——————

3/4 lb. boneless trimmed beef sirloin steak
3/4 lb. pork loin tenderloin
1 large red bell pepper, seeded
1 large green bell pepper, seeded
2 fresh green chili peppers
1 (8-oz.) can tomatoes
1 (8-oz.) can pimentos, drained
2 tablespoons fresh lemon juice
2 tablespoons olive oil
1 garlic clove, crushed
1 teaspoon ground turmeric
1/2 to 1 teaspoon salt
1/2 teaspoon freshly ground black pepper
Fresh flat-leaf parsley sprigs to garnish

Cut meat in 1-inch cubes. Cut peppers in 1-inch pieces. To prepare marinade, process remaining ingredients to a paste in a food processor fitted with a metal blade. In a medium-size saucepan, simmer marinade until reduced by half. Cool and pour into a large bowl. Stir in meat and bell peppers. Cover tightly and refrigerate 12 hours.

Thread meat and bell peppers onto skewers, alternating red and green bell pepper pieces. Cook on a rack over hot coals about 20 minutes or until meat is to desired doneness, turning skewers frequently and basting with marinade. Garnish with parsley sprigs. Makes 5 to 6 servings.

Note: If desired, serve with corn or taco chips and Spicy Almonds, page 107.

Drunken Roast Pork

1 (3-lb.) boneless rolled pork roast
2 tablespoons butter
1 large onion, chopped
2 carrots, peeled, thinly sliced
2 celery stalks, finely sliced
1 large leek, sliced
2/3 cup dry red wine
1 tablespoon chopped fresh thyme leaves
2 teaspoons chopped fresh tarragon leaves
Salt and black pepper to taste
2 tablespoons dry sherry
Fresh thyme sprigs and tarragon sprigs to
    garnish
2 tablespoons brandy

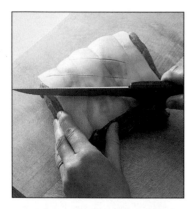

Score through outside of roast at 1-inch intervals. Tie with string in several places.

Place roast on a spit or in a covered barbecue. Cook over low coals about 2 hours. If not using a spit, turn roast every 15 minutes to ensure even cooking. Meanwhile, to prepare sauce, melt butter in a medium-size saucepan. Saute onion until brown, then add carrots, celery, leek, wine and herbs. Cover pan and simmer until vegetables are very soft, stirring occasionally. Strain through a sieve or process to a liquid in a food processor fitted with a metal blade. Return to pan and season with salt and pepper. Stir in sherry.

When roast reaches 170F (75C) in center, place on a hot flame-proof serving platter. Reserve several thyme and tarragon sprigs. Pierce meat in several places and insert remaining thyme and tarragon sprigs. Pour brandy into a metal ladle and heat gently over barbecue a few seconds until warm. Pour over roast and immediately ignite. Reheat sauce and spoon brandied juice into sauce. Slice roast. Garnish with reserved thyme and tarragon sprigs and serve with sauce. Makes 6 to 8 servings.

Beef in Tahini Paste

1-1/2 lbs. boneless beef top sirloin steak
1/4 cup tahini paste
1/2 cup sesame seed oil
1/2 teaspoon garlic salt
1 tablespoon lemon juice
Freshly ground black pepper to taste
8 green onions, finely chopped
3 tablespoons sesame seeds, toasted
Green onion flowers to garnish

Cut beef across grain in 20 to 25 thin slices.

To prepare sauce, combine tahini paste, sesame seed oil, garlic salt and lemon juice in a small bowl. Season with pepper and stir in chopped green onions. Using tongs, dip slices of beef, 1 at a time, into sauce, then spread on a tray. Cover with plastic wrap or foil. Refrigerate at least 1 hour. Reserve sauce.

Cook beef on a rack over hot coals 30 seconds. Turn beef over and brush with reserved sauce. Cook 1 to 1/2 minutes more or to desired doneness. Arrange beef on a hot platter. Sprinkle with sesame seeds and garnish with green onion flowers. Makes 6 to 7 servings.

Steak & Seafood Platter

**4 (6-oz.) boneless beef top sirloin steaks, about
    1 inch thick
1/2 lb. peeled cooked medium-size shrimp
2 garlic cloves
1/4 teaspoon salt
1/2 cup butter
1 tablespoon plus 1 teaspoon paprika
1/4 teaspoon hot-pepper sauce
1/4 cup whipping cream
4 unpeeled cooked large shrimp and 4 green
    leaf lettuce leaves to garnish**

Using a fork, pierce steaks on both sides. Blot
peeled shrimp with paper towels.

In a small bowl, crush garlic with salt. In a
small saucepan, combine salted garlic, butter,
paprika and hot-pepper sauce. Warm gently
over minimum heat until butter is very soft
but not liquified. Stir in whipping cream and
remove from heat.

Brush steaks on both sides with butter mixture. Fold peeled shrimp into remaining butter mixture. Cook steaks on a rack over hot
coals 1 minute on each side to seal. Continue
cooking to desired doneness, see page 11,
turning steaks over occasionally. When steaks
are nearly done, heat pan of shrimp on side of
rack 2 or 3 minutes or until hot. Spoon hot
shrimp on top of steaks. Garnish with unpeeled shrimp and lettuce leaves. Makes 4
servings.

Vermont Pork Chops

4 (1-inch-thick) pork chops
4 green onions, trimmed, finely sliced
2 garlic cloves, very finely chopped
1/4 cup maple syrup
1 tablespoon plus 1 teaspoon ketchup
1 cup unsweetened apple juice
1/8 teaspoon chili powder
1/8 teaspoon ground cinnamon
1/8 teaspoon finely ground black pepper
1 teaspoon salt
8 to 12 shelled pecans, dipped into maple
    syrup, and green onion flowers to garnish

Trim surplus fat from chops and pierce on
both sides.

To prepare marinade, combine sliced green
onions, garlic, maple syrup, ketchup, apple
juice, chili powder, cinnamon, pepper and
salt in a large shallow dish. Stir briskly to
thoroughly blend in ketchup. Add chops,
turning to coat both sides. Cover and refrigerate at least 2 hours, turning chops over once
or twice.

Cook chops on a rack over medium coals 15 to
20 minutes on each side or until no longer
pink in center, basting frequently with marinade. Just before serving, spoon remaining
marinade over chops, evenly distributing any
green onions in bottom of dish. Garnish with
pecans and green onion flowers. Makes 4
servings.

Note: This is delicious served with roasted
sweet potatoes.

Lamb with Cheese Sauce

3/4 lb. lean ground lamb
1 egg, beaten
1 teaspoon dried leaf rosemary
1/2 cup fresh white bread crumbs
1 small red bell pepper, seeded, minced
1 teaspoon hot-pepper sauce
1/2 teaspoon onion salt
1/2 teaspoon freshly ground black pepper
Fresh rosemary sprigs to garnish

Cheese Sauce:
1-1/2 teaspoons butter
1 tablespoon all-purpose flour
1/2 cup milk
1 egg yolk
1/3 cup dairy sour cream
2 ozs. Lancashire cheese, crumbled

In a medium-size bowl, combine ground lamb, egg, dried rosemary, bread crumbs, bell pepper, hot-pepper sauce, onion salt and pepper. Shape mixture in 16 rectangular fingers. Refrigerate 30 minutes.

Meanwhile, to prepare Cheese Sauce, melt butter in a small saucepan. Stir in flour. Remove from heat and thoroughly blend in milk. Cook over moderate heat until sauce thickens to consistency of thin cream, stirring constantly. Remove pan from heat. In a small bowl, blend egg yolk with sour cream. Pour into sauce. Stir in cheese. Cook over medium heat 3 to 4 minutes or until cheese has melted. Do not overheat or sauce will curdle. Cover to keep warm.

Cook lamb fingers on an oiled rack over hot coals 5 to 6 minutes on each side or to desired doneness, reducing heat if lamb becomes too brown. Arrange 4 lamb fingers in a fan shape on each plate. Spoon sauce over tips, allowing sauce to form a pool. Garnish with rosemary. Makes 4 servings.

Bacon Lattice Steaks

4 (8-oz.) sirloin steaks, about 1 inch thick
4 slices bacon
Freshly ground black pepper to taste
1/4 cup olive oil
Fresh flat-leaf parsley sprigs to garnish

Using a sharp knife, make 3 deep diagonal slashes lengthwise and 3 slashes crosswise on each side of steaks, but do not cut through.

Cut bacon in thin strips. Insert bacon strips into slashes to form a lattice. Press with palm of hand. Season steaks with pepper. Brush all over with olive oil.

Cook steaks on a rack over hot coals 1 minute on each side to seal. Continue cooking to desired doneness, see page 11, turning steaks over occasionally. Garnish with parsley sprigs. Makes 4 servings.

Note: Serve with coleslaw.

Vitello Sirotti

8 (6-oz.) veal cutlets
3 tablespoons butter, softened
12 pitted olives, chopped
1/2 cup pine nuts, finely chopped
1-1/4 cups soft bread crumbs
Salt and freshly ground black pepper to taste
Fresh flat-leaf parsley sprigs to garnish

Sauce:
1 (14-oz.) can tomatoes
1 garlic clove
1 handful fresh parsley sprigs
1 tablespoon olive oil
1/4 cup plus 2 tablespoons dry red wine

Beat cutlets until thin between sheets of waxed paper.

In a small bowl, combine butter, olives, pine nuts and bread crumbs. Season with salt and pepper. Mix well. Spoon a portion of butter mixture on 1 edge of each cutlet and roll up, jelly-roll style.

Securely wrap each cutlet in a well oiled double thickness of foil. Cook foil packets on a rack over medium coals in a covered barbecue 20 minutes or until tender. Or cook 30 to 45 minutes or until tender in an uncovered barbecue. Turn foil packets over halfway through cooking. Meanwhile, to prepare sauce, process all sauce ingredients to a liquid in a food processor fitted with a metal blade. Strain through a nylon sieve into a small saucepan. Cook over moderate heat until sauce thickens, stirring constantly. Cover and keep warm. Garnish veal with parsley sprigs and serve with sauce. Makes 8 servings.

Mexican Muffins

4 (3-oz.) beef fillet steaks, about 1/2 inch thick
1 large or 2 small ripe but firm avocados
1/2 cup crumbled Danish Mycella or other blue
    cheese (2 ozs.)
2 teaspoons fresh lemon juice
2 English muffins, split
Cayenne pepper

Cook steaks on a oiled rack over hot coals 1
minute on each side to seal. Continue cooking
to desired doneness, see page 11, turning
steaks over occasionally.

Meanwhile, cut avocados in half. Remove pit
and scoop out flesh. Using a fork, mash avo
cado, cheese and lemon juice in a small bowl.
Toast muffins on both sides on rack.

When steaks are nearly done, spread with 1/2
of avocado mixture. When done, cover with
toasted muffin halves, then invert onto hot
serving plates. Top with a dollop of remaining avocado mixture and sprinkle with cayenne pepper. Makes 4 servings.

Note: Do not prepare avocado mixture in
advance or color will darken.

Lamb Chops with Tamarind

3 tablespoons butter
1 medium-size onion, finely chopped
2 tablespoons tamarind concentrate
2 tablespoons tomato paste
1 (1-inch) piece gingerroot, finely grated
2 teaspoons dark-brown sugar
2 tablespoons olive oil
Grated peel and juice 1 large orange
6 thick loin pork chops
Orange segments, orange peel strips and fresh
    parsley sprigs to garnish

To prepare sauce, melt butter in a small saucepan. Saute onion until soft.

Stir in tamarind concentrate, tomato paste, gingerroot, brown sugar, olive oil and grated orange peel and juice. Simmer gently, uncovered, 7 to 8 minutes or until mixture is reduced by one-fourth. Cool and pour into a large shallow dish. Coat chops thoroughly in sauce. Cover and refrigerate overnight.

Cook chops on a rack over hot coals 15 to 20 minutes, turning twice during cooking and basting frequently with remaining sauce. If there is not sufficient sauce for basting, use a little olive oil. Garnish with orange segments, orange peel and parsley. Makes 6 servings.

Note: Serve with Sage & Sour Cream Jackets, page 83.

—— Venison with Blueberry Sauce ——

6 (4-oz.) venison steaks
Grated peel and juice 2 oranges
Juice 1 lemon
3 tablespoons bourbon whiskey
1/2 cup olive oil
1 teaspoon dried rosemary leaves
1 teaspoon celery salt
3 bay leaves
Fresh blueberries, bay leaves and orange slices,
    cut in quarters, to garnish

Blueberry Sauce:
1 cup light-brown sugar
1 tablespoon fresh lemon juice
2/3 cup water
8 ozs. fresh blueberries, rinsed, stems removed

On a flat surface, flatten steaks with a mallet or rolling pin.

To prepare marinade, combine orange peel and orange and lemon juices, whiskey, olive oil, rosemary and celery salt in a large shallow dish. Add bay leaves. Coat both sides of steaks in marinade. Cover and refrigerate 6 to 8 hours, basting occasionally. To prepare Blueberry Sauce, combine brown sugar, lemon juice and water in a small saucepan. Simmer until brown sugar is dissolved, stirring frequently. Stir blueberries into syrup and bring to a boil. Reduce heat and cook until mixture is pulpy, stirring frequently.

Cook steaks on an oiled rack over hot coals about 10 seconds per side to seal. Brush steaks with marinade. Continue cooking 5 to 7 minutes side or until tender. Garnish steaks with blueberries, bay leaves and orange pieces and serve with sauce. Makes 6 servings.

Chicken St. Lucia

1/4 cup water
1 cup creamed coconut, grated
1 teaspoon ground cumin
1 teaspoon ground cardamom
1/4 cup mango chutney
1/2 cup corn oil
1/2 teaspoon salt
1 tablespoon plus 1 teaspoon turmeric
4 (10- to 12-oz.) chicken quarters
Fresh flat-leaf parsley sprigs to garnish

To prepare sauce, heat water in a small sauce-pan. Stir in coconut. When well blended, re-move from heat. Stir in cumin, cardamom and chutney. Spoon mixture into a bowl and cover.

In a small bowl, combine oil, salt and turmer-ic. Brush generously all over chicken. Cook chicken on a rack over medium coals 12 to 15 minutes on each side, basting frequently with remaining seasoned oil. To test for doneness, pierce through to bone with a skewer to make sure that juices are clear.

Garnish with parsley sprigs and serve with sauce. Makes 4 servings.

Cranberry Ballotine

1 (4-lb.) broiler-fryer chicken
2 tablespoons vegetable oil
1 medium-size onion, chopped
1/2 cup uncooked long-grain rice
1 cup hot chicken stock
1/2 cup dark raisins
Grated peel and juice 1 lemon
Salt and black pepper to taste
1 egg, beaten
2 ozs. fresh or frozen cranberries, cooked,
    drained
1/2 teaspoon sugar
Additional fresh cranberries, lemon peel, and
    fresh flat-leaf parsley sprigs to garnish

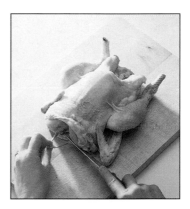

Remove chicken wings at second joint and
reserve. Loosen skin at neck, cut around wish
bone and remove.

Cut through skin and flesh along backbone.
Carefully cut flesh away from bone. Sever
shoulder joint, ease carcass out. Push back
skin from thighs. Cut away flesh and turn
inside out. Repeat for wing bones. Spread
skin out on work surface and cover evenly
with flesh. Heat oil in a medium-size saucepan. Saute onion until soft. Add rice, chicken
stock, raisins and lemon peel and juice. Cover
and simmer 20 minutes or until stock is
absorbed.

Season with salt and pepper. Cool, then beat
in egg. Spread rice mixture over flesh side of
chicken, leaving a 3/4-inch border. In a small
bowl, combine cranberries and sugar. Spoon
lengthwise along center of rice mixture.
Reshape chicken and sew with strong thread.
Cook on a rack over low coals in a covered
barbecue 1 to 1-1/4 hours or until chicken is
dark-golden brown. Let stand 10 to 15 minutes and carve in slices. Garnish with additional cranberries, lemon peel and parsley
sprigs. Makes 6 to 7 servings.

Chicken Teriyaki

1-1/2 lbs. skinned boneless chicken breasts
3 (8-oz.) cans water chestnuts, drained
1/4 cup dry sherry
1/4 cup dry white wine
1/4 cup soy sauce
2 garlic cloves, crushed
Sunflower oil
Shredded lettuce
Onion rings, paprika and fresh flat-leaf parsley
    sprigs to garnish

Cut chicken in 1-inch cubes. In a medium-size dish, combine chicken and water chestnuts.

To prepare marinade, combine sherry, wine, soy sauce and garlic in a small bowl. Pour over chicken and water chestnuts. Cover and refrigerate 1 hour, stirring occasionally. Using a slotted spoon, remove chicken and water chestnuts from marinade. Alternately thread chicken and water chestnuts onto 8 skewers.

Brush chicken and water chestnuts with sunflower oil. Cook on a rack over hot coals about 10 minutes, turning frequently and basting with remaining marinade and sunflower oil. Arrange shredded lettuce on a large serving platter. Place skewers in a criss-cross pattern on lettuce. Garnish with onion rings, a dash of paprika and parsley sprigs. Makes 8 servings.

Chicken Liver Kebabs

1-1/4 lbs. chicken livers, rinsed, trimmed
1/4 cup sunflower oil
1 medium-size onion, finely chopped
1 garlic clove, crushed
1/4 cup dry red wine
1/2 teaspoon hot-pepper sauce
1-1/2 teaspoons dark-brown sugar
12 black peppercorns
Salt to taste
18 canned water chestnuts, cut in half
1 large red bell pepper, seeded, cut in rings
Fresh flat-leaf parsley sprigs to garnish

Cut chicken livers in half.

To prepare marinade, heat sunflower oil in a small saucepan. Saute onion until soft. Add garlic, wine, hot-pepper sauce, brown sugar and peppercorns. Season with salt. Bring to a boil. Add livers and simmer 1 minute to firm liver. Remove from heat. Transfer livers to a medium-size bowl. Cover and refrigerate 2 hours.

Using a slotted spoon, remove livers from marinade. Alternately thread livers and water chestnuts onto 6 skewers. Remove and discard peppercorns from marinade. Cook on a rack over hot coals 6 to 8 minutes, turning frequently and basting occasionally with marinade. Toss bell pepper rings with remaining marinade and serve with kebabs. Garnish with parsley. Makes 6 servings.

Hickory Smoked Chicken

2 handfuls hickory smoking chips
Handful of mixed fresh herbs
1 (3- to 4-lb.) broiler-fryer chicken
Salt to taste
Fresh flat-leaf parsley sprigs, radishes, cut in half, and lettuce leaves to garnish

Soak hickory chips in hot water. Light a covered barbecue or wet smoker. When coals are hot, drain hickory chips. Sprinkle hickory chips over hot coals. Place a water pan in barbecue.

Sprinkle herbs in a heat-proof pan or dish of hot water. Place a rack over pan and set over hot coals. Season chicken with salt. Place chicken on rack and close barbecue cover.

Reduce heat and cook chicken over low coals about 3 hours, turning chicken every 30 minutes. If necessary, add hot water to water pan during cooking. To add water, move chicken to one side and add water with extreme caution. When cooked, chicken should be moist with faintly pink-tinged flesh and a distinctive smoky flavor. Garnish with parsley sprigs, radishes and lettuce. Makes 4 to 6 servings.

Mango Chicken

2 medium-size mangos
Juice 1/2 small lime
1 tablespoon mango chutney
1/2 cup salted butter, softened
1 tablespoon fresh lemon juice
Pinch ground ginger
Pinch cayenne pepper
Pinch ground cloves
Pinch salt
6 (4-oz.) skinned boneless chicken breasts
Lime twists to garnish

Cut mangos lengthwise from top to bottom as close to pit as possible.

Cut fruit away from pit. Peel, then thinly slice fruit lengthwise. Finely chop 2 ounces of less attractive slices to use in mango butter. Sprinkle remaining slices with lime juice. To prepare mango butter, thoroughly blend finely chopped mangos, chutney, butter, lemon juice, ginger, cayenne pepper, cloves and salt.

Cut small horizontal slits in both sides of chicken breasts. Insert mango butter into each slit. Melt remaining mango butter in a small saucepan. Cook chicken on a rack over hot coals 7 to 8 minutes on each side, basting frequently with mango butter. Garnish with reserved mango slices and lime twists. Makes 6 servings.

Chicken Satay

1-1/2 lbs. skinned boneless chicken breast
2/3 cup unsalted skinless peanuts, roasted
2 tablespoons walnut oil
1 large onion, finely chopped
3 garlic cloves, finely chopped
1 (7-oz.) bar creamed coconut
2 cups hot water
2 tablespoon fresh lemon juice
2 teaspoons salt
1 teaspoon ground cardamom
1/2 teaspoon ground ginger
2 teaspoons ground turmeric
Lemon wedges

Cut chicken in 1-inch cubes. Grind peanuts finely in a food processor fitted with a metal blade.

To prepare marinade, heat walnut oil in a medium-size skillet. Saute onion and garlic until soft. In a large bowl, blend creamed coconut with hot water. Stir in ground peanuts, lemon juice, salt, cardamom, ginger and turmeric. Add onion and garlic, including any oil left in pan. Add chicken and stir well. Cover and refrigerate 4 hours.

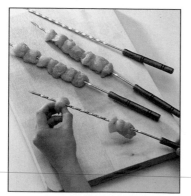

Using a slotted spoon, remove chicken from marinade. Thread onto 8 skewers. Cook on a rack over hot coals 10 to 12 minutes, turning frequently and basting with remaining marinade. Serve with lemon. Makes 8 servings.

Note: Serve with shrimp chips which may be purchased from selected grocers and Japanese or Asian food stores. Deep fry chips up to 1 day ahead and store in an airtight container. Garnish with fresh flat-leaf parsley sprigs.

Deep South Drumsticks

12 to 16 chicken drumsticks
1/4 cup plus 2 tablespoons tomato paste
3 tablespoons dry red wine
Juice 1/2 lemon
2 tablespoons Worcestershire sauce
2 tablespoons dark molasses
1 teaspoon salt
1/2 teaspoon black pepper
1 teaspoon prepared mustard
1 teaspoon chili powder
1 teaspoon paprika
2 tablespoons vegetable oil
1 slice whole-wheat bread, crust removed,
    diced
Fresh flat-leaf parsley sprigs and pickled
    miniature ears of corn to garnish

Wash and dry drumsticks.

To prepare sauce, combine remaining ingredients in a large shallow dish. Stir with a
fork until bread is incorporated. Sauce will be
thick. Place drumsticks in sauce, twisting at
bone end to coat evenly. Cover and refrigerate 1 hour, turning drumsticks occasionally.

Wrap each drumstick in an oiled single thickness of foil. Cook on a rack over medium coals
30 to 40 minutes, turning foil packets occasionally. Test 1 drumstick for doneness.
Juices should run clear and flesh touching
bone be fully cooked. Garnish with parsley
sprigs and corn and serve in foil. Makes 6 to 8
servings.

Chicken Tartlets

2 lbs. skinned boneless chicken breasts
Fresh bay leaves to garnish

Paté:
1/2 lb. chicken livers, rinsed, cut in half
1/4 cup dry sherry
2 tablespoons water
1/4 teaspoon ground mace
1 bay leaf
1 teaspoon salt
1/4 teaspoon freshly ground black pepper
1-1/2 cups butter, coarsely chopped
2 teaspoons brandy

Brush a 12-cup muffin tin with oil a few hours in advance. Do not use a nonstick tin. Pound chicken breasts 1/8 inch thick between pieces of waxed paper. Cut flattened chicken in rounds to fit oiled cups. Fit rounds into oiled cups. Trim away surplus scraps to use in paté. Place a small piece of oiled foil on each round. Cover and refrigerate.

To prepare paté, put chicken trimmings and livers into a large saucepan. Add sherry, water, mace, bay leaf, salt and pepper. Cover and simmer gently 5 to 7 minutes or until both chicken and livers are cooked. Remove and discard bay leaf. In a blender, process hot mixture with butter and brandy. Pour into a 1-1/4-cup dish. Cover and refrigerate until firm. Place muffin tin on a rack over medium coals. Cook until chicken is opaque and underside is slightly brown. Loosen from cup with a round-tipped knife and fill with paté. The paté will soften due to heat of chicken. Garnish with bay leaves. Makes 12 servings.

Tandoori Turkey

6 (6-oz.) skinned boneless turkey breasts
Juice 3 small lemons
3/4 cup plain yogurt
1/2 cup vegetable oil
4 garlic cloves, crushed
2 teaspoons paprika
2 teaspoons ground cumin
1 tablespoon plus 1 teaspoon ground turmeric
1/2 teaspoon ground ginger
2 teaspoon salt
Few drops red food coloring, if desired

Cut deep slashes in turkey breasts on both sides. Place in a single layer in a large shallow dish.

In a small bowl, combine lemon juice, yogurt, oil, garlic, paprika, cumin, turmeric, ginger and salt. Blend well. If desired, tint with a few drops of red food coloring to give a deep orange-red color. Pour over turkey breasts. Turn turkey breasts over, coating both sides. Cover and refrigerate at least 12 hours.

Cook turkey on an oiled rack over hot coals 10 minutes on each side until cooked through, basting frequently with marinade. Makes 6 to 8 servings.

Note: Serve with a tomato and onion salad, garnished with fresh flat-leaf parsley sprigs, and Cucumber Raita, page 105.

Butter Cream Chicken

1 (2-1/2-lb.) broiler-fryer chicken
3 tablespoons butter, softened
3/4 teaspoon grated lemon peel
3/4 teaspoon dry mustard
1/2 cup whipping cream
Fresh flat-leaf parsley sprigs to garnish

On a flat surface, cut chicken through back-bone using a sharp knife. with skin side up, flatten chicken to 1 inch thick using a mallet or rolling pin.

In a small bowl, combine butter, lemon peel, mustard and whipping cream. Spread chicken with 1/2 of butter cream. Diagonally inset 2 long skewers through both thighs and breast, crossing them over in center.

Cook on a rack over hot coals 20 minutes, basting occasionally with remaining butter cream and turning once. Reduce heat and move chicken to side of rack. Continue cook-ing about 20 minutes or until juices run clear, turning once. Remove skewers and cut in fourths. Garnish with parsley sprigs. Makes 4 servings.

Chicken Aioli

5 garlic cloves
2 egg yolks
1/2 cup olive oil
1 teaspoon fresh lemon juice
1 teaspoon water
Salt and freshly ground black pepper to taste
2 (2-lb.) broiler-fryer chickens
Lemon slices and fresh flat-leaf parsley sprigs
   to garnish

In a medium-size bowl, smash garlic to a pulp with a pestle. Gradually beat in egg yolks.

To prepare garlic mayonnaise, beat olive oil into egg mixture drop by drop until mixture begins to thicken. In a 1-cup measure, combine lemon juice and water. Beat into olive oil mixture until well incorporated. Season with salt and pepper. Mix well.

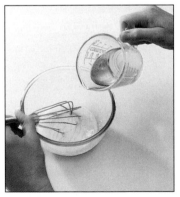

Loosen skin of chicken and spread garlic mayonnaise close to flesh. Brush garlic mayonnaise inside cavity and over outside of chicken. Wrap each chicken in a double thickness of foil. Cook on a rack over medium coals 30 minutes. Remove chickens from foil. Cook chickens on rack 15 to 20 minutes more, turning occasionally and basting with remaining garlic mayonnaise. Cut chickens in half. Garnish with lemon slices and parsley. Makes 4 servings.

— Spit Roast Duck with Cherry Sauce —

1 (4-1/2-lb.) duckling
Salt and freshly ground black pepper to taste
2/3 cup pineapple juice

Sauce:
1 lb. pitted fresh black cherries
1 garlic clove
2/3 cup port wine
1-3/4 cups strong beef stock
1 tablespoon potato flour
2 tablespoons cold water
2 tablespoons butter
1 tablespoon red currant jelly
Salt and freshly ground black pepper to taste
Fresh black cherries and fresh flat-leaf parsley
    to garnish

Prick duck through skin in several places. Season inside and out with salt and pepper. Sprinkle inside with some pineapple juice.

To prepare sauce, combine cherries, garlic, wine and beef stock in a large saucepan. Simmer until cherries are tender. Remove cherries with a slotted spoon. Remove and discard garlic. In a 1-cup measure, blend potato flour and cold water. Stir into liquid in pan. Bring to a boil, stirring continuously until thickened. Mix in butter and jelly. Season with salt and pepper. Add cherries and cook until hot.

Light barbecue and when coals are hot, move coals towards side. Place a roasting pan or foil dish large enough to catch drips in center. Fix duck onto a spit or put into a wire rack set in a pan. Cook over medium coals 2-1/4 to 3 hours or until well done. Tenting with foil or cooking in a covered barbecue will hasten cooking. Do not open cover for 30 minutes, then baste every 10 minutes with remaining pineapple juice. Remove duck. Pour off fat and mix juices into hot sauce. Garnish duck with cherries and parsley sprigs and serve with sauce. Makes 6 to 8 servings.

Applejack Duck

4 (1-lb.) duck breast quarters
1-1/4 cups thawed frozen apple juice
**   concentrate**
1-1/4 cups water
2 teaspoons ground cloves
2 teaspoons dried leaf oregano
1 teaspoon salt
1/2 teaspoon freshly ground black pepper
Lemon wedges and fresh flat-leaf parsley
**   sprigs to garnish**

Using a sharp knife, diagonally score through
skin and flesh of duck, creating a diamond
pattern. Place skin side down in a large glass
dish.

In a medium-size bowl, combine remaining
ingredients. Pour over duck. Cover and refrigerate at least 6 hours or overnight.

Cook on a rack over medium coals about 1-1/4
hours, turning every 20 minutes and basting
with remaining marinade. Tenting with foil
or cooking in a covered barbecue will hasten
cooking. Garnish with lemon wedges and
parsley sprigs. Makes 4 servings.

Note: Serve with Walnut Apple Crescents,
page 85.

Ginger & Apricot Chicken

8 to 10 chicken thighs
1 (14-1/2-oz.) can apricot halves in natural juice
About 1 cup fresh orange juice
1 tablespoon walnut oil
1 tablespoon minced onion
1 teaspoon grated gingerroot
Salt and freshly ground black pepper to taste
16 fresh sweet red cherries, pitted
Additional fresh sweet red cherries to garnish

Deeply slash chicken thighs to bone in 2 or 3 places.

To prepare marinade, drain juice from apricots into a 2-cup measure. Add enough orange juice to make 1-1/2 cups. Reserve 16 apricots for garnish and mash remaining apricots. In a large bowl, combine juice, mashed apricots, walnut oil, onion and gingerroot. Season with salt and pepper. Add chicken, turning to coat. Cover and refrigerate 2 hours, stirring occasionally.

Cook chicken on an oiled rack over hot coals 25 to 30 minutes, turning 2 or 3 times and basting with remaining marinade. Place reserved apricots on a foil tray on rack 5 minutes or until warm. Fill apricots with cherries and serve with chicken. Garnish with additional cherries. Makes 4 servings.

Piquant Spring Chicken

2 (2-lb.) broiler-fryer chickens
3/4 cup tomato juice
1/4 cup Worcestershire sauce
2 teaspoons fresh lemon juice
Juice 1/2 orange
Freshly ground black pepper to taste
4 medium-size heads Belgian endive
Butter
Salt to taste
Thin orange slices, cut in quarters, to garnish

Cut chickens in half so that each half has a wing and a leg. Place cut-side up in a large shallow dish.

To prepare marinade, combine tomato juice, Worcestershire sauce, and lemon and orange juices in a medium-size bowl. Season with pepper. Mix well. Pour over chicken. Cover and refrigerate 12 hours, basting occasionally. Place each head of endive on a piece of a double thickness of foil. Dot with butter and season with salt and pepper. Wrap tightly.

Cook chicken on an oiled rack over medium coals 30 to 40 minutes or until juices run clear when cut, basting occasionally with remaining marinade. Cook foil packets over or in medium coals during final 10 to 12 minutes of cooking. Garnish chicken with orange pieces and serve with endive cut in half lengthwise. Makes 4 servings.

Sunday Chicken Brunch

12 chicken livers, rinsed
1/4 cup vegetable oil
Salt and white pepper to taste
4 (4-oz.) skinned boneless chicken breasts
4 eggs
3 tablespoons milk
1 tablespoon butter
Toast triangles and cherry tomatoes to garnish

Pat livers with paper towels to remove surplus moisture. Thread onto 4 oiled skewers, leaving a small gap between each liver. Season oil with salt and pepper. Mix well. Brush over livers.

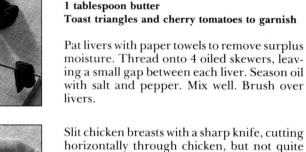

Slit chicken breasts with a sharp knife, cutting horizontally through chicken, but not quite severing. Open out and brush with seasoned oil. Cook chicken on a rack over hot coals 6 to 10 minutes on each side, basting occasionally. Add skewered livers last 8 to 10 minutes of cooking, brushing with seasoned oil and turning skewers frequently.

Meanwhile, beat eggs and milk in a small bowl. Season with salt and pepper. Mix well. Melt butter in a small saucepan on side of rack. Scramble eggs in butter. Spoon scrambled eggs over chicken. Remove livers from skewers with a fork. Top eggs with livers. Garnish with toast triangles and cherry tomatoes. Makes 4 servings.

Chinese Duck

3 (1-lb.) duck breast quarters
2 teaspoons miso paste
1/3 cup dry sherry or saki (rice wine)
1/4 to 1/2 teaspoon five-spice powder
2 cups all-purpose flour
3/4 cup boiling water
Sesame oil
Hoisin sauce
1 bunch green onions, trimmed,
    shredded lengthwise
Green onion flowers to garnish

Deeply score duck flesh through to bone in a criss-cross fashion. Place in a large shallow dish. To prepare marinade, blend miso paste, sherry and five-spice powder in a small bowl. Cover duck with marinade, spreading marinade spreads under skin. Cover and refrigerate at least 12 hours, basting occasionally.

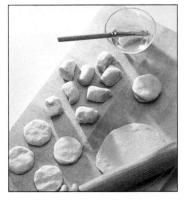

To prepare pancakes, place flour in a large bowl. Gradually pour in boiling water and beat to form a dough. Knead 10 minutes. Cover with a damp cloth and let stand 30 minutes. Knead again 5 minutes, then form dough in a sausage shape. Divide in 16 equal pieces. Working with 2 pieces of dough at a time, lightly press each piece to a 2-inch circle. Oil 1 side of each piece of dough, then sandwich 2 oiled sides together. With a rolling pin, roll dough to 7-inch circles. Cook in large skillet over low heat about 1 to 1-1/2 minutes per side. When cooked, peel halves. Cook duck on a rack over low coals in a covered barbecue about 1 hour, turning duck over 3 times during cooking and basting with remaining marinade.

Shred meat from bone while duck is still hot. Serve duck with pancakes, hoisin sauce and shredded green onions. Garnish with green onion flowers. Makes 3 to 4 servings.

Capered New Potatoes

1 lb. medium-size new potatoes, scrubbed
3 tablespoons capers, finely chopped
1/3 cup butter, softened
Fresh flat-leaf parsley sprigs to garnish

In a large saucepan, boil potatoes in skins in salted water 10 minutes. Drain and cool slightly.

In a small bowl, blend capers with butter. Make a deep slit in each potato and fill with caper butter.

Tightly wrap each potato separately in foil. Cook on a rack over hot coals 10 to 15 minutes or until tender. Garnish with parsley sprigs. Makes 6 servings.

Note: Capered New Potatoes are ideal as an accompaniment with plain grilled fish or poultry.

Whole Tomatoes in Wine

8 medium-size firm tomatoes
2 tablespoons plus 2 teaspoons dry red wine
Salt and freshly ground black pepper to taste
Green leaf lettuce leaves or watercress

Cup each tomato in a double thickness of foil, but do not completely enclose.

Pour 1 teaspoon of wine over each tomato. Season with salt and pepper. Securely mold foil around tomatoes to prevent juices from escaping.

Cook foil packets on side of a rack over medium coals about 10 to 15 minutes. Unwrap and transfer to serving plates, spooning wine flavored juices over tomatoes. Serve on lettuce leaves. Makes 8 servings.

Note: These tomatoes are particularly delicious as an accompaniment to barbecued steaks or burgers which can be cooked at the same time.

Hot Hot Aloo

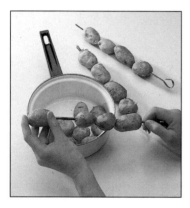

1 lb. small new potatoes, scrubbed
1/4 cup lime pickle, exactly measured
1/4 cup vegetable oil
2 teaspoons tomato paste
2 teaspoons ground cardamum
2 tablespoons plain yogurt
Lime slices to garnish

In a large saucepan, boil potatoes in skins in salted water until tender but firm. Drain. Cool and thread onto 4 to 6 skewers.

Place lime pickle in a small bowl. Using kitchen scissors, snip any large pieces of lime pickle. Blend in oil, tomato paste, cardamum and yogurt.

Spoon pickle mixture over skewered potatoes to coat each potato. Cook on a rack over hot coals about 10 minutes, turning frequently. Garnish with lime. Makes 4 to 6 servings.

Note: If desired, substitute mild lime pickle for lime pickle.

Sweet & Sour Eggplant

2 medium-size eggplants
3 tablespoons tarragon vinegar
3 tablespoons olive oil
Small garlic clove, crushed
Pinch salt
1/2 teaspoon prepared mustard
1 tablespoon chopped fresh parsley
1/2 teaspoon dried leaf marjoram
Pinch cayenne pepper
1 tablespoon sugar
Fresh marjoram sprigs to garnish

Peel eggplant and cut in half. Slice and cut in 1-inch cubes.

Combine remaining ingredients in a large bowl. Add cubed eggplant and mix well. Let stand 15 minutes, stirring occasionally.

Thread onto 8 skewers. Cook over hot coals 15 minutes, turning occasionally. Garnish with marjoram sprigs. Makes 8 servings.

Note: Serve with grilled steaks or chops.

Country Mushrooms

12 fresh jumbo mushrooms, wiped clean
1/4 cup virgin olive oil
1/4 cup fresh lemon juice
1 tablespoon plus 2 teaspoons grated fresh
  horseradish
1/4 teaspoon salt
1/4 teaspoon freshly ground black pepper
1 tablespoon chopped fresh parsley
Fresh flat-leaf parsley sprigs to garnish

If necessary, cut mushroom stalks to 1/2 inch
in length.

Thoroughly mix olive oil, lemon juice,
horseradish, salt and pepper in a large shallow dish. Add mushrooms, spooning liquid
over to completely coat mushrooms. Let
stand 30 minutes, basting occasionally.

Cook on a rack over hot coals about 10 minutes, turning over and basting occasionally.
To serve, sprinkle open sides of mushrooms
with chopped parsley. Garnish with parsley
sprigs. Makes 4 to 6 servings.

Charcoaled Spanish Onions

2 large Spanish onions
Garlic salt
1/4 cup whipping cream, half whipped
1 tablespoon crushed black peppercorns
2 tablespoons butter
Fresh rosemary sprigs to garnish

Peel onions and slice in 1/2-inch-thick slices. Do not separate in rings.

Season with garlic salt. Brush 1 side with whipping cream and sprinkle with crushed peppercorns.

Place cream-side up in a hinged meat grill. Tent with foil. Cook over hot coals 5 to 8 minutes per side or until beginning to "charcoal." Dot onions with butter while cooking. Serve peppered side up. Garnish with rosemary sprigs. Makes 4 to 6 servings.

Note: Serve with meat, with other vegetables or as an appetizer.

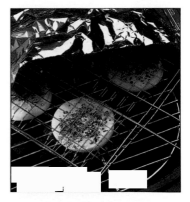

Singed Spiced Plantains

6 underripe plantains or bananas
2 tablespoons butter, softened
2 tablespoons lemon juice
1/2 teaspoon ground allspice
Pinch ginger
Lemon slices to garnish

Without peeling, cook bananas over medium coals until skin blackens, turning frequently.

In a small bowl, combine butter, lemon juice, allspice and ginger.

Cut cooked bananas in half lengthwise. Spoon spicy butter over bananas. Garnish with lemon. Makes 6 servings.

Note: Serve with chicken, gammon or veal.

Sage & Sour Cream Jackets

6 medium-size baking potatoes, scrubbed
Vegetable oil
2 tablespoons white wine vinegar
1 bunch green onions, finely sliced
1 egg yolk
Pinch dry mustard
Salt and pepper to taste
1 teaspoon finely chopped fresh sage leaves
2/3 cup dairy sour cream
Fresh sage leaves, to garnish

Prick potatoes deeply through skins and rub with oil.

Wrap each potato in a double thickness of foil. Bake in coals 45 minutes to 1 hour or until soft, turning occasionally.

In a small saucepan, combine vinegar and green onions. Cook over low heat until vinegar has almost evaporated. Remove pan from heat. In a small bowl, beat egg yolk and dry mustard. Season with salt and pepper. Mix well. Stir into green onions. Cook over very low heat 1 minute or until mixture thickens, beating constantly. Do not overheat or sauce may curdle. Remove pan from heat and stir in chopped sage leaves and sour cream. When potatoes are done, cut a deep cross through foil and squeeze sides of potatoes to open. Spoon sauce into potatoes. Serve in foil wrappings. Garnish with sage. Makes 8 servings.

Zucchini with Garden Herbs

8 to 10 (5-inch-long) young firm zucchini,
   washed, ends removed
1 teaspoon fresh lemon verbena leaves
4 to 5 fresh mint leaves
1 teaspoon fresh marjoram leaves
1/2 teaspoon salt
2 tablespoons dry white wine
2 tablespoons fresh lemon juice
1/4 cup sunflower oil
2 bay leaves
Lemon slices and fresh lemon verbena, mint or
   marjoram sprigs, to garnish

Pierce zucchini at either end and in 1 or 2
places along length. Finely chop lemon verbena, mint and marjoram.

In a large bowl, mix herbs, salt, wine, lemon
juice and sunflower oil. Add zucchini and bay
leaves, turning zucchini over to coat thoroughly. Cover and refrigerate 4 to 5 hours,
tossing occasionally in marinade.

Remove zucchini from marinade. Cook on a
rack over hot coals about 8 to 10 minutes or
until tender but not soft, turning frequently
and basting with remaining marinade. Serve
skewered with wooden sticks. Garnish with
lemon slices and lemon verbena sprigs.
Makes 8 to 10 servings.

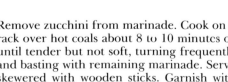

Walnut Apple Crescents

2 small Red Delicious apples, rinsed, dried
1/4 cup apple juice
1 teaspoon grated orange peel
1/3 cup shelled walnuts, coarsely chopped
1/4 cup coarsely chopped dates
Orange peel strips and walnut halves to
    garnish

Remove apple core, keeping apples whole.
Cut each apple in half lengthwise. Each half
will have a tubular-shape hollow along center.

In a small saucepan, combine apple juice,
grated orange peel, walnuts and dates. Bring
to a boil, then simmer 2 to 3 minutes or until
liquid has been absorbed. Cool slightly, then
fill apple hollows with walnut mixture.

Wrap each apple half in a double thickness of
foil. Cook on a rack over hot coals about 30
minutes or until apples are tender, turning
occasionally. Garnish with orange peel strips
and walnuts. Makes 4 servings.

Note: Serve as an accompaniment with poultry or game.

Skewered Potato Crisps

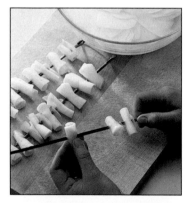

2 (8-oz.) baking potatoes, peeled
1/4 cup sunflower oil

Carefully cut potatoes in paper thin slices lengthwise, following curve of potato.

Immediately plunge potato slices into hot salted water. Stir to separate, then let stand 3 to 4 minutes or until pliable. Carefully coil each potato slice, then thread onto skewers, leaving at least 1/2-inch space between coils.

Brush potato coils with sunflower oil. Cook on a rack over hot coals 10 to 15 minutes or until potato coils are crisp, turning frequently. Drain on paper towels to remove excess oil. Makes 8 to 10 servings.

Note: To double this recipe, soak 1/2 of potato slices in a separate bowl.

Vegetable Bar

8 ozs. evenly shaped carrots
1 medium-size cauliflower
3 ears fresh corn
1 tablespoon milk
1/2 lb. Chinese snow peas, ends removed
1/2 lb. pearl onions, peeled
Vegetable oil

Using a small paring knife, cut carrots in chunks and shape in barrels. Separate cauliflower in flowerettes.

Cut corn in 1-inch slices using a heavy sharp knife. Fill a large saucepan with water. Add milk and bring to a boil. Separately plunge vegetables and cook al dente. Drain in a colander under cold running water. Arrange vegetables in separate serving bowls.

Thread vegetables on 8 to 10 skewers. Baste with oil. Cook on a rack over hot coals 5 minutes, turning skewers frequently. Makes 8 to 10 servings.

Note: Serve with Mild Tomato Sauce, page 108, and Leek & Bacon Sauce, page 109.

Crusty Garlic Potatoes

8 to 10 large garlic cloves
1 lb. new potatoes, scrubbed
2 eggs, beaten
1/2 cup yellow corn meal
Fresh flat-leaf parsley sprigs to garnish

Peel garlic leaving cloves whole.

In a large saucepan, boil garlic and potatoes in salted water 12 to 15 minutes or until potatoes are just tender. Drain and reserve garlic. Cool potatoes and remove skin. Coarsely chop garlic. Using a small skewer, insert garlic pieces deeply into potatoes.

Dip potato in beaten eggs, then in corn meal. Press well with a round-bladed knife, then dip in beaten eggs again. Cook on a well-oiled rack over hot coals 10 to 15 minutes or until crusty and golden. Garnish with parsley sprigs. Makes 5 to 6 servings.

Peanut Tomatoes

8 fried bread bracelets
Vegetable oil
4 large tomatoes, rinsed, cut in half
Salt and freshly ground black pepper to taste
Few drops Worcestershire sauce
2 teaspoons chopped fresh basil
2 teaspoons chopped fresh parsley
1/4 cup freshly grated Parmesan cheese
1/3 cup roasted unsalted peanuts, finely ground
Butter
Fresh basil sprigs to garnish

To prepare bracelets, cut 8 rounds from 8 slices of bread. Use a slightly small cutter to remove centers. Fry bracelets in shallow oil. Drain thoroughly on paper towels.

Season cut surfaces of tomatoes with salt and pepper.

Sprinkle with Worcestershire sauce. In a small bowl, combine basil and parsley. Sprinkle tomatoes with herb mixture, then sprinkle with Parmesan cheese. Cover with ground peanuts. Dot with butter. Loosely wrap tomato halves in foil. Place cut-side up on a rack. Cook over hot coals 20 to 25 minutes or until tomatoes are soft. Place each tomato in center of a fried bread bracelet. Garnish with basil. Makes 4 to 8 servings.

Note: Bracelets can be crispened on barbecue. If desired, prepare bracelets and freeze until needed.

Stuffed Eggplant

6 (6-oz.) eggplants
2 tablespoons butter
1 medium-size onion, finely chopped
1 garlic clove, crushed
1 (8-oz.) can tomatoes
1/3 cup fresh bread crumbs
1/2 cup grated Cheddar cheese (2 ozs.)
1 teaspoon dried leaf oregano
Salt and freshly ground black pepper to taste
Sprigs of fresh oregano to garnish

Trim stem ends from eggplants. Cut a thin slice from lengths of eggplants and reserve. Scoop out flesh from eggplant, leaving 1/4-inch shell. Finely chop flesh.

Melt butter in a medium-size saucepan. Saute onion and garlic in butter until soft. Add chopped eggplant and fry until eggplant is tender. Remove from heat. Stir in tomatoes with juice, bread crumbs, cheese and dried oregano. Season with salt and pepper. Mix well.

Pack filling into eggplant shells. Replace reserved eggplant slices. Wrap each eggplant in a lightly oiled double thickness of foil. Cook on a rack over medium coals or cook in coals 20 to 30 minutes. Garnish with oregano sprigs. Makes 6 servings.

Roast Corn-on-the-Cob

6 ears fresh corn with husks
1/2 cup butter, melted
Fresh flat-leaf parsley sprigs and chives
**   to garnish**

Herbed Butter:
1/4 cup butter, softened
1 teaspoon fresh lemon juice
2 tablespoons chopped fresh parsley
1 tablespoon chopped chives
Salt and pepper to taste

Fold back corn husks. Remove silk from corn and re-wrap husks over corn. Soak in cold water at least 1 hour. Drain and shake off surplus water.

Meanwhile, to prepare Herbed Butter, beat all ingredients in a small bowl until softened and well blended. Roll in a 1-inch cylinder. Wrap tightly in waxed paper. Chill in freezer until firm, then slice. Arrange in a single layer on a plate and refrigerate until needed.

Pull back husks and brush corn with melted butter. Rewrap in husks. Cook on a rack over medium coals 30 to 40 minutes or until husks are well-browned, turning frequently. Remove husks and serve corn with Herbed Butter slices. Garnish with parsley sprigs and chives. Makes 6 servings.

Potato & Egg Stuffed Peppers

4 small green bell peppers
4 hard-cooked eggs, peeled, coarsely chopped
1/2 lb. cooked potatoes, coarsely chopped
3 tablespoons mayonnaise
2 teaspoons prepared mustard
1 tablespoon plus 1 teaspoon chopped fresh
   chives
1 teaspoon paprika
1/2 teaspoon garlic salt
Freshly ground black pepper to taste
Fresh flat-leaf parsley sprigs to garnish

Cut a thin slice from stalk end of each bell pepper. Remove core, seeds and membrane.

In a large bowl, combine eggs, potatoes, mayonnaise, mustard, chives, paprika and garlic salt. Season with pepper. Mix well.

Carefully spoon potato mixture into bell peppers. Wrap each bell pepper in a lightly buttered double thickness of foil. Cook on a rack or in medium coals about 30 minutes or until bell peppers are tender, turning foil packets over occasionally. Garnish with parsley sprigs. Makes 4 servings.

Note: Serve with Mild Tomato Sauce, page 108.

Brazil Nut Burgers

3 tablespoons butter
1 medium-size onion, finely chopped
1 celery stalk, finely chopped
1/2 small green bell pepper, finely chopped
1/2 lb. shelled Brazil nuts, finely ground
1 medium-size carrot, peeled, grated
1 teaspoon yeast extract
1-1/4 cups vegetable stock
1/4 cup plus 2 tablespoons bulgar
Salt and freshly ground black pepper to taste
2 eggs, beaten
All-purpose flour
Vegetable oil
Green bell pepper rings, to garnish

Melt butter in a large saucepan. Saute onion, celery and bell pepper in butter until soft. Stir nuts into mixture and cook 3 to 4 minutes, stirring constantly. Stir in carrot, yeast extract and vegetable stock. Bring to a boil, then simmer 5 minutes. Mix in bulgar. Season with salt and pepper. Mix well. Cool, then bind with beaten eggs to consistency of a thick paste.

Shape in 6 to 7 burgers. Dust with flour. Place burgers on a well-oiled foil tray. Place tray on a rack and cook over hot coals 10 minutes, turning burgers over once during cooking. Burgers may brown unevenly, but this gives a more "barbecued" appearance. Makes 6 to 7 servings.

Note: Serve with Mild Tomato Sauce, page 108.

Green Lentil Zucchini

3 large firm zucchini, cut in half lengthwise
2 green onions, finely sliced
1 small green bell pepper, cored, seeded, finely
   chopped
1 medium-size tomato, peeled, chopped
1/2 cup cooked green lentils
1 teaspoon fresh basil leaves, snipped
Salt and freshly ground black pepper to taste
2 tablespoons grated roasted hazelnuts
Sprigs of fresh basil to garnish

Scoop zucchini pulp into a large bowl, leaving
a 1/4-inch shell. Reserve shells.

Add green onions, bell pepper and tomatoes
to zucchini pulp. Mix in lentils and snipped
basil. Season with salt and pepper. Mix well.

Place each zucchini half on a large square of a
double thickness of foil. Pile mixture high
into reserved shells. Wrap securely, leaving a
space above stuffing for steam to circulate.
Cook on a rack over hot coals about 20 minutes or until zucchini are tender but firm.
Open packets and sprinkle with hazelnuts.
Garnish with basil. Makes 6 servings.

Broccoli Pancake Rolls

1/2 lb. fresh broccoli, cooked, drained, finely
    chopped
1/3 cup plain yogurt
Freshly ground black pepper to taste
2 tablespoons all-purpose flour
3 tablespoons milk
4 large eggs
1 tablespoon soy sauce
Butter
Vegetable oil
Fresh flat-leaf parsley sprigs and green leaf
    lettuce leaves to garnish

In a medium-size bowl, combine broccoli and yogurt. Season with pepper. Cover and set aside.

Sift flour into another medium-size bowl. Blend in milk. In a small bowl, beat eggs and soy sauce. Gradually add to flour mixture, beating well to a smooth thin batter. Heat a small omelette pan. Butter pan. Prepare 6 to 8 (6-inch) thin pancakes, browning on 1 side only. Remove pancakes carefully (they set as they cool). Place cooked side up on waxed paper.

Spoon a small amount of broccoli filling onto center of browned side of each pancake. Fold to enclose filling, tucking in sides. Fold again to form a packet. Brush cool pancake rolls with oil. Cook over hot coals 3 to 4 minutes on each side, starting with seam side down. Garnish with parsley sprigs and lettuce leaves. Makes 6 to 8 servings.

Note: Serve with a green salad or couscous.

Celery & Stilton Avocado

3 ripe avocados
2 tablespoons lemon juice
Salt and freshly ground black pepper to taste
2 celery stalks, cooked, chopped
1/2 cup cooked brown rice
3/4 cup crumbled white Stilton cheese (3 ozs.)
1 tablespoon tomato paste
Pinch chili powder
Seedless red grapes, cut in half, and fresh celery leaves to garnish

Cut avocados in half and remove pits. Pour lemon juice into a small dish. Season with salt and pepper. Mix well. Brush over cut surfaces of avocado.

Place avocado halves cut-side up on an oiled foil tray. In a medium-size bowl, combine celery, brown rice, cheese, tomato paste and chili powder. Pile in avocado halves.

Place foil tray on a rack. Tent loosely with foil or cook in a covered barbecue over medium coals 15 to 20 minutes or until heated through. Garnish with grape halves and celery leaves. Makes 6 servings.

Kiwifruit & Stem Ginger

6 firm kiwifruit, rinsed
5 to 6 tablespoons ginger syrup
6 pieces stem ginger in syrup, cut in half
** lengthwise**
1 tablespoon chopped shelled pistachio nuts
Stem ginger slices to garnish

Cut kiwifruit in half lengthwise. Remove firm core, chop and reserve. Spoon ginger syrup over kiwifruit. Pierce with a skewer to help absorption.

Place stem ginger in cavities in kiwifruit. Place each filled kiwifruit on a square of foil. Spoon a small amount of ginger syrup over stem ginger. Wrap securely.

Cook over medium hot coals 10 to 15 minutes, turning foil packets over towards end of cooking time. Open packets and sprinkle cutside of kiwifruit with reserved chopped core and nuts. Garnish with stem ginger slices. Makes 6 servings.

Grand Marnier Kebabs

3 firm fresh apricots
3 firm fresh figs
2 (1-inch) pineapple slices
2 tangerines
2 firm bananas
2 Delicious apples
1 tablespoon fresh lemon juice
1/3 cup unsalted butter
1/2 cup powdered sugar
1 tablespoon Grand Marnier
1 tablespoon fresh orange juice
1 tablespoon finely grated orange peel

Cut apricots in half and remove pits. Remove stalks and cut figs lengthwise in quarters.

Remove any woody core and cut pineapple slices in chunks. Peel tangerines and cut in quarters, but do not remove membranes. Peel bananas and cut in 1-inch-thick slices. Peel apples and cut in quarters. Remove core and cut each quarter crosswise. Sprinkle apples and bananas with lemon juice.

Thread a mixture of fruit onto 6 to 8 skewers, starting and finishing with apple and pineapple. To prepare sauce, melt butter in a small saucepan. Stir in powdered sugar, then Grand Marnier and orange juice and peel. Brush kebabs with sauce. Cook over medium coals 5 to 6 minutes, basting frequently with sauce. Serve hot with remaining sauce. Makes 6 servings.

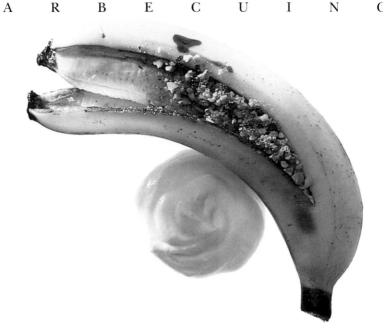

Praline Bananas

2 tablespoons shelled unskinned almonds
2 tablespoons shelled unskinned hazelnuts
1/4 cup sugar
6 medium-size underripe bananas
Whipped cream

Line a baking sheet with waxed paper. In a small skillet, combine almonds, hazelnuts and sugar. Heat gently until sugar dissolves, stirring constantly. Increase heat and cook to a deep-brown syrup. Immediately pour hot toffee-like mixture onto prepared baking sheet. Let stand until cold and brittle, then break up in pieces. In a food processor fitted with a metal blade, process praline pieces to a powder.

Cut 1 slit through banana skins along top surface. Slightly open and fill slit with about 1 tablespoon of praline. Reshape bananas and wrap each banana tightly in a double thickness of foil, sealing along top.

Cook on medium coals 8 to 10 minutes, turning foil packets over half-way through cooking time. Unfold foil wrapping and slightly open banana skins. Serve with whipped cream. Makes 6 servings.

Peaches & Butterscotch Sauce

6 medium-size peaches, washed
1/2 cup ground almonds
2 tablespoons finely chopped angelica
Angelica "leaves" to garnish

Butterscotch Sauce:
1/2 cup light-brown sugar
2/3 cup maple syrup
3 tablespoons butter
Pinch salt
2/3 cup half and half
2 teaspoons vanilla extract

Cut peaches in half. Remove pits.

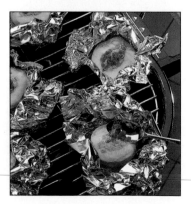

To prepare Butterscotch Sauce, combine brown sugar, maple syrup, butter and salt in a small saucepan. Bring to a boil, stir once, then boil 3 minutes or until a thick syrup forms. Stir in half and half. Bring back to a boil and immediately remove from heat. Stir in vanilla. Cover and keep warm.

Place each peach half cut-side down on a square of a double thickness of foil. Fold up sides of foil, but do not seal. Cook on a rack over hot coals 5 minute. Open foil packets and turn peaches over. Spoon ground almonds and chopped angelica into cavities. Top with 1 tablespoon of Butterscotch Sauce. Draw up edges of foil and twist above peaches to seal. Cook 10 minutes or until peaches are tender. Garnish with angelica "leaves" and serve hot with remaining sauce. Makes 6 to 12 servings.

Vodka Soused Pineapple

3 tablespoons vodka
4 (3/4-inch-thick) pineapple slices
1/3 cup unsalted butter
1/4 cup whipping cream
1 teaspoon ground cardamom
2 tablespoons powdered sugar
12 sour black cherries
Additional powdered sugar
Pineapple leaves to garnish

Pour vodka into a shallow dish. Add pineapple slices, turning over to coat. Cover and refrigerate 20 minutes.

Melt butter in a small saucepan. Stir in whipping cream, cardamom and 2 tablespoons powdered sugar.

Dip pineapple slices into butter mixture. Cook on a rack over hot coals 5 minutes on each side or until golden brown. Place on heated plates. Fill pineapple centers with cherries and dust lightly with additional powdered sugar. Garnish with pineapple leaves. Makes 4 servings.

Rum & Raisin Persimmons

6 ripe persimmons
2 tablespoons finely chopped mixed dried fruit
1 glacé cherry, finely chopped
3 shelled almonds, finely chopped
2 teaspoons dark-brown sugar
1 teaspoon dark rum
Pinch ground cinnamon
1/2 teaspoon fresh lemon juice
6 small fresh strawberries to garnish

Remove stems from persimmons. Using a teaspoon, scoop out pulp into a medium-size bowl, leaving fleshy wall intact.

Mix dried fruit, cherry, almonds, brown sugar, rum, cinnamon and lemon juice into persimmon pulp. Carefully pack filling into persimmon shells. Wrap each persimmon in a lightly oiled double thickness of foil.

Place foil packets in medium coals. Cook 25 to 30 minutes or until persimmons are soft. Unwrap and garnish with strawberries. Makes 6 servings.

Hot Tropicanas

3 medium-size pink grapefruit
8 medium-size lychees
2 medium-size kumquats, rinsed, dried
1 medium-size guava
1 medium-size papaw
1 small mango
1/4 cup light corn syrup
2 tablespoons butter
2 tablespoons toasted sweetened shredded
     coconut
Fresh mint sprigs to garnish

Cut grapefruit in half. Remove segments and drain. Scrape out grapefruit shells, discarding membranes.

Peel lychees and remove pits. Slice kumquats. Cut guava and papaw in half. Scoop out seeds, then peel and dice flesh. Peel mango and cut flesh away from pit. Cut flesh in strips. Combine all fruit in a large bowl. Melt corn syrup in a small saucepan. Pour over fruit and mix gently.

Spoon fruit mixture into grapefruit shells. Dot with butter. Wrap each grapefruit half in a large piece of double thickness of foil. Cook on a rack over medium coals 7 to 10 minutes or until fruit is warm but not cooked. Remove grapefruit from foil. Place in individual dishes and sprinkle with toasted coconut. Garnish with mint sprigs. Makes 6 servings.

Pear & Peach Apples

2 dried pear halves
2 dried peach halves
1 tablespoon golden raisins
1/8 teaspoon ground cloves
Pinch ground allspice
1/3 cup light-brown sugar, softened
2 tablespoons butter, softened
4 medium-size cooking apples
Unsweetened whipped cream

Place pear and peach halves in a medium-size saucepan. Cover with water, bring to a boil and cook 5 minutes. Drain thoroughly, then chop. In a medium-size bowl, combine chopped fruit, raisins, cloves, allspice, brown sugar and butter.

Wash and core apples. Pack apple cavities firmly with fruit filling. Place each apple on a square of a double thickness of foil. Draw up edges of foil and twist firmly to secure above apples.

Cook on a rack over medium coals 45 to 50 minutes or until apples are tender. Using twisted foil as an aid, turn apples on their sides several times. Or cook in coals without turning 20 to 30 minutes or until apples are tender. Snip off foil stalks. Fold wrapping back to expose apples, keeping apples nestled in foil. Serve with whipped cream. Makes 4 servings.

Cucumber Raita

1 small cucumber, peeled, finely chopped
1 teaspoon salt
2-1/2 cups plain yogurt
1 teaspoon finely chopped onion
1 teaspoon chopped fresh cilantro
Black pepper to taste
Fresh cilantro sprigs to garnish

Line a nylon sieve with a thick fold of paper towels. Place cucumber in prepared sieve. Sprinkle with salt and let stand 1 hour to drain.

Line another sieve with muslin. Set over a bowl and spoon in yogurt. Refrigerate 2 hours.

Discard whey from yogurt. In a medium-size bowl, combine drained cucumber, yogurt, onion and chopped cilantro. Season with pepper. Mix well. Garnish with cilantro sprigs. Makes 8 servings.

Potters Red Relish

4 large ripe tomatoes
1 small red bell pepper, cored, seeded
1 small green bell pepper, cored, seeded
1 large onion
2 teaspoons salt
1/2 cup dark-brown sugar
2/3 cup malt vinegar
1/2 teaspoon sweet paprika
Fresh flat-leaf parsley sprigs to garnish

Peel tomatoes and finely chop. Very finely chop red and green peppers and onion.

In a large saucepan, combine chopped vegetables and remaining ingredients. Bring to a boil. Reduce heat and simmer gently 1 hour or until mixture is thick, stirring frequently.

Spoon into a large sterilized jar and cover with a sterilized lid. Refrigerate 1 to 2 weeks before using. To serve, garnish with parsley sprigs. Makes about 2 cups.

Spicy Almonds

1/2 lb. shelled almonds
1/4 teaspoon ground allspice
1/4 teaspoon ground cumin
2 teaspoons salt
3 tablespoons butter

Place almonds in a medium-size saucepan of hot water. Bring to a boil. Reduce heat and simmer 30 seconds. Drain. Let stand 1 minute, then rub off skins. In a small bowl, mix allspice, cumin and salt.

Melt butter in a medium-size skillet. Saute almonds until brown.

Drain on paper towels. While hot, sprinkle with spiced salt and toss to coat almonds on all sides. Cool, place in a strainer and shake to remove surplus salt. Makes 1-1/2 cups.

Mild Tomato Sauce

2 tablespoons olive oil
1 celery stalk, finely chopped
1 medium-size onion, finely chopped
1 (14-oz.) can tomatoes
1 teaspoon sugar
1 teaspoon snipped fresh basil leaves
1 teaspoon chopped fresh parsley
Salt and freshly ground black pepper to taste
1 teaspoon butter
Fresh basil sprig to garnish

Heat olive oil in a medium-size saucepan until hot. Saute celery and onion until soft.

Stir in tomatoes with juice, sugar, basil leaves and parsley. Cover and simmer 20 minutes. Remove cover and cook 10 minutes more. Press mixture through a sieve into a medium-size bowl. Discard seeds, herbs and celery strings.

Wash pan and return sauce to pan. Reheat sauce. Season with salt and pepper and stir in butter. Garnish with basil sprig. Makes 1-1/4 cups.

Leek & Bacon Sauce

**14 ozs. firm leeks, cleaned, trimmed, finely
 sliced**
2 strips bacon
2/3 cup plain yogurt
1/4 teaspoon cayenne pepper
Freshly ground black pepper to taste

In a large saucepan, simmer leaks in salted
water until soft. Drain.

Cook bacon on a rack over hot coals until
cooked but not crisp.

Cut up bacon. In a blender, process leeks,
bacon and yogurt to a puree. Add cayenne
pepper and season with black pepper. Mix
well. Serve warm as a sauce or cold as a dip.
Makes 2 cups.

Note: If using as a dip, sprinkle with crisp
crumbled bacon.

Chive & Garlic Bread

1 loaf French bread
3 garlic cloves
1/4 teaspoon salt
1/2 cup butter, softened
2 tablespoons chopped fresh chives

Slice bread diagonally and deeply at 3/4-inch intervals but do not cut completely through.

Place garlic on a piece of waxed paper. Sprinkle with salt and crush with flat side of a knife. In a small bowl, combine salted garlic, butter and chives. Spread garlic butter between slices of bread, generously covering both sides.

Reshape loaf and wrap securely in foil. Cook on a rack over hot coals 10 to 15 minutes, turning foil packet over several times. Open foil and separate slices. Serve at once. Makes 6 servings.

Pasta & Bean Salad

1 small red bell pepper, cored, seeded
1 small green bell pepper, cored, seeded
1/2 cup cooked green beans, sliced diagonally
1/2 cup cooked kidney beans
6 ozs. pasta bows, cooked, drained
1/2 lb. bean sprouts, rinsed, drained
Fresh flat-leaf parsley sprig to garnish

Dressing:
1/2 cup olive oil
2 tablespoons fresh lemon juice
2 teaspoons soy sauce
1/2 teaspoon salt
1/4 teaspoon freshly ground black pepper
3 tablespoons fresh chopped parsley

Cook bell peppers on a rack over hot coals 7 minutes or until charred and blistered, turning occasionally. Peel peppers. Cut in half lengthwise, then cut in thin strips.

Place bell peppers, green beans, kidney beans, pasta and bean sprouts in a serving bowl. To prepare dressing, combine all dressing ingredients in a 1-cup measure. Pour over salad ingredients and toss well. Garnish with parsley sprig. Makes 6 servings.

Crispy Potato Skins

4 large baking potatoes, scrubbed
1/2 cup butter
Salt and freshly ground black pepper to taste

Prick potatoes in several places. Wrap tightly in foil. Cook in hot coals 45 to 60 minutes or until soft.

Cut potatoes in half lengthwise and scoop out pulp. Reserve pulp for another use. Cut potato skins in 1-inch-wide strips.

Melt butter in a small saucepan and season with salt and pepper. Dip potato skins into seasoned butter and thread onto skewers. Cook on a rack over hot coals 5 to 7 minutes or until crisp. Serve hot. Makes 6 to 8 servings.

Note: Potatoes can be baked in a preheated oven at 425F (220C) 1 hour—do not wrap in foil. After dipping potato skin strips into seasoned butter, skins can be spread on a baking sheet and baked in a preheated oven at 450F (230C) 5 to 10 minutes or until crisp.

Watercress Salad

2 (1/2-inch-thick) slices white bread
1/2 garlic clove
Vegetable oil
Green lettuce leaves
2 bunches fresh watercress, rinsed, drained
2 tablespoons mayonnaise
1/4 cup vinaigrette dressing

Remove crusts and cut bread into small cubes.

Rub garlic over inside of a medium-size skillet. Discard garlic. Pour 1/2 inch of oil into skillet. Heat oil and add bread cubes. Fry until golden brown. Remove with a slotted spoon and drain on paper towels. If necessary, prepare bread cubes in 2 batches.

Line a serving bowl with lettuce leaves. Trim coarse stalks or any discolored leaves from watercress. In a small bowl, combine mayonnaise and vinaigrette dressing. Toss watercress in dressing mixture. Arrange watercress on lettuce leaves and top with croûtons. Makes 4 to 6 servings.

Fennel Salad

12 radishes, trimmed
3 medium-size fennel bulbs
1 Green Delicious apple, cored, diced
2 medium-size carrots, peeled, cut in thin
    julienne strips
1 tablespoon lemon juice
1/4 cup plus 2 tablespoons mayonnaise

Make vertical cuts in radishes on 4 sides. Soak in ice cold water 2 to 3 hours or until "petals" open. Drain and reserve for garnish.

Trim fennel and reserve fern-like leaves. Cut bulbs in half, discarding any hard core. Slice thinly. In a large bowl, combine sliced fennel, apple and carrots. Mix in lemon juice, then stir in mayonnaise until well blended.

Spoon into a serving bowl. Garnish with radish flowers and reserved fennel leaves. Makes 4 to 6 servings.

Orange Rice Salad

1 (11-oz.) can mandarin oranges in natural
   juice
About 2 cups orange juice
1-1/4 cups white long-grain rice, rinsed
1 teaspoon butter
1 teaspoon salt
2 canned whole pimentos, well drained, cut in
   strips
1 small onion, finely chopped
1/4 lb. fresh Chinese snow peas, ends removed,
   sliced diagonally
2 ozs. peeled cooked shrimp, coarsely chopped
1/4 cup plus 1 tablespoon olive oil
2 tablespoons cider vinegar
Pinch sugar
Pinch dry mustard
1/2 teaspoon black pepper
Unpeeled cooked shrimp to garnish

Drain juice from oranges. Reserve oranges.
Add enough orange juice to mandarin
orange juice to measure 2-1/4 cups. In a large
saucepan, combine orange juice, rice, butter
and 1/2 teaspoon of salt. Bring to a boil and
stir once. Reduce heat, cover and simmer 15
minutes or until rice is tender and orange
juice is absorbed. Spoon rice into a medium-
size bowl and fluff with a fork. Cool.

In a bowl, combine rice, pimentos, onion,
snow peas and chopped shrimp. To prepare
dressing, whisk olive oil, cider vinegar, sugar,
dry mustard, pepper and remaining salt.
Carefully toss salad with dressing. Garnish
with reserved oranges and shrimp. Makes 6
servings.

MENU ONE

Juniper Crown Roast, page 38
Capered New Potatoes, page 76
Zucchini with Garden Herbs, page 84
Hot Tropicanas, page 103

MENU TWO

Frankfurters with Mustard Dip, page 42
Pasta & Bean Salad, page 111
Orange Rice Salad, page 115
Kiwifruit & Stem Ginger, page 97

MENU THREE

Chicken Teriyaki, page 60
Vegetable Bar, page 87
Chive & Garlic Bread, page 110
Vodka Soused Pineapple, page 101

MENU FOUR

Cranberry Ballotine, page 59
Sage and Sour Cream Jackets, page 83
Fennel Salad, page 114
Peaches & Butterscotch Sauce, page 100

INDEX